Journeys Through Our Classrooms

. . .

Edited by
Denis Udall and Amy Mednick

KENDALL/HUNT PUBL
4050 Westmark Drive D

D0814265

Cover Photo: Jackie Phillips, a kindergartner at the Rocky Mountain School of Expeditionary Learning (Denver), during an expedition on the human body. Photo
by David L. Cornwell.

Expeditionary Learning^{SM} is a Service Mark of Outward Bound, Inc.
Outward Bound® is a Registered Trademark of Outward Bound, Inc.

Dedication

To our colleagues in Expeditionary Learning
Outward Bound schools,
with admiration and appreciation.

Table of Contents

Foreword

Eleanor Duckworth

I spoke with several ten-year-olds in the streets of a small East Coast city. They went to a school three blocks from the harbor front. I mentioned the ocean, I can't remember why, and learned from them that they had never seen it. It's true that there were buildings between their school and the water; it is also possible that the children simply didn't realize that what they had seen was the ocean. But one way or the other, that school was letting them down.

This collection celebrates teachers' capacity to use what is available for teaching, beyond the textbooks and worksheets that have come to define what it means to learn in school. "What is available" is an understatement. What education is about is helping our youngsters learn about the world and how it works. The world itself is the subject of study—the world itself and ways of living in it. That is what these teachers have grasped.

It is also what they have struggled with. None of these is a story of easy accomplishment. Each of the teachers had to explore new territory—decide what part of the world she or he could open for students; locate resources and ways of using them that would engage their students; find ways to encourage students in taking initiatives that were new to them; resolve countless new classroom issues that arose from doing things in a different way; and help parents and colleagues appreciate the importance of the work.

And there is a further concern in each of these accounts—a concern shared explicitly by all the teachers, and by the organization that pulls them together here. Each teacher keeps a central focus on maintaining a classroom in which students develop a respect for each other—for each other's ways and each other's ideas.

The triumph of this collection is that a great range of teachers, in a great range of classrooms and schools, has managed to do this, in a great variety of different ways. Each story is compelling. Together they hold out hope that our schools may, after all, be able to find ways of educating our young people for the very complicated world in which we find ourselves.

Acknowledgments

Expeditionary Learning Outward Bound would like to thank the following funders who have made our work possible: Americorps; the DeWitt Wallace-Readers' Digest Foundation; the J.M. Kaplan Fund; the Geraldine R. Dodge Foundation; the Edna McConnell Clark Foundation; the Dragon Foundation; the Surdna Foundation; and the Starr Foundation. Finally, we are especially grateful to New American Schools Development Corporation for its generous support and guidance.

Expeditionary Learning would also like to thank the following people for giving their time and support in enriching this book: Annie Adamsky, Kim Archung, Mark Bowen, David Duncan, Greg Farrell, Vivian Fung, Daphne Leslie Harris, Harold Howe II, Mieko Kamii, Doug Kilmister, Raïssa Lerner, Elizabeth Maynard, Steve Seidel, and Margo Shearman. Casey Cheung contributed to the design of the book.

"Making Theater, Making Sense, Making Change" was originally commissioned by Expeditionary Learning Outward Bound, a version also appeared in *Social Issues and Service at the Middle Level,* Samuel Totten and Jon E. Pedersen (Eds.), Needham, Massachusetts; Allyn and Bacon (1995). "Something From Nothing: An Expedition into Economy, Community and History" was originally commissioned by Expeditionary Learning Outward Bound, a version also appeared in *Starting From Scratch: One Classroom Builds its Own Curriculum* by Steven Levy; Heinemann (1996). "The World is Mine. Soon. I Hope." first appeared in *Writing Within School Reform,* Grace Hall McEntee and Joseph Check (Eds.). Annenberg Institute for School Reform (1995). Copyright © 1995 by Loretta Brady. Reprinted with permission. "Are We There Yet?: Immersion Journalism as a Discussion of Good Work" first appeared in *More Than The Truth: Teaching Non-Fiction Writing Through Journalism*, Dennie Palmer Wolf and Julie Craven with Dana Balick (Eds.). Copyright © 1996 by Heinemann. A version has been reprinted with permission.

Introduction

Denis Udall and Leah Rugen

At first encounter, the phrase *expeditionary learning* conjures up images of backpacking and mountain climbing. But the founders of Expeditionary Learning Outward Bound (see Appendix) drew on the metaphor of a wilderness expedition to develop a framework for curriculum design (prekindergarten–twelfth grades). During "learning expeditions," teachers and students pursue long-term intellectual investigations built around significant projects and performances. These investigations take students out into the world and bring the world into the classroom, and often provide students with opportunities to serve the wider community. A learning expedition is marked by equal attention to intellectual inquiry, character development, and community building, with opportunities for ongoing assessment woven throughout, pushing students to higher levels of achievement.

This book assembles the stories of teachers who, for the past several years, have been immersed in creating and teaching curriculum that takes the form of such expeditions. Within the growing network of Expeditionary Learning Outward Bound, the active exchange of teaching practices and the close consideration of students' work has been at the core of teachers' professional development. This book is meant to enrich these conversations, as well as inspire other educators involved in transforming schools and classrooms into places of challenge and compassion.

Key Design Principles

To imagine whole schools in which all learning is seen as an expedition—a journey with a purpose—Expeditionary Learning Outward Bound has articulated ten design principles (see Appendix). They speak to nearly every dimension of the life of a school. The principles are stated in language uncommon in schools. For example, the first principle, *The Primacy of Self-Discovery*, points to integrating the intellect and character: "Learning happens best with emotion, challenge, and the requisite support. People discover their abilities, values, 'grand passions,' and responsibilities in situations that offer adventure and the unexpected. They must have tasks that require perseverance, fitness, craftsmanship, imagination, self-discipline, and significant achievement. A primary job of the educator is to help students overcome their fear and discover they have more in them than they think."

Another principle, *Intimacy and Caring,* states: "Learning is fostered best in small groups where there is trust, sustained caring, and mutual respect among all members of the learning community. Keep schools and learning groups small. Be sure there is a caring adult looking after the progress of each child. Arrange for the older students to mentor the younger ones." It underlies the relationships and structures that allow the first principle to unfold.

Going beyond the focus on trust and respectful relationships to consider the core intellectual focus of teaching and learning, another principle, *The Having of Wonderful Ideas,* inspired by Eleanor Duckworth's essay (1987), points to learning that awakens the thinking of both students and teachers: "Teach so as to build on children's curiosity about the world by creating learning situations that provide matter to think about, time to experiment, and time to make sense of what is observed. Foster a community where students' and adults' ideas are respected."

Philosophical and poetic, these principles provoke and inspire a school community to reflect on its core mission and values from the vantage of the learners' experience. They must be interpreted and applied to be useful, and they speak as much to a school's relationships and ethos as to its curricula and teaching practices. The teacher narratives that make up this book examine the evolution of teaching and curriculum in schools and classrooms that take such principles seriously.

About This Book

For the past several years Expeditionary Learning staff have been listening closely and assisting Expeditionary Learning teachers in documenting their planning and teaching of learning expeditions. We have also been observing, talking with, and collecting the stories of teachers outside our network who have created and taught intellectual learning expeditions for years. Thus, the reader will find two types of stories in this book. One kind is written by teachers themselves. Several of these authors come from outside our network of schools and have inspired Expeditionary Learning since its inception. The second kind, by Expeditionary Learning teachers with the assistance of Expeditionary Learning staff, is based mainly on transcribed interviews.

It might be important to say what this book is not. Readers expecting a step-by-step, "how-to" manual or curriculum guide will be disappointed. That does not mean teachers will not find valuable ideas or activities they can use in their classrooms, but that is not this book's primary intention. Instead, the authors have very different purposes in mind. First, they want their readers, as colleagues, to join them in rethinking teaching and learning, and they hope that their stories are useful to faculties and teams as a starting point for ongoing conversations about practice. Second, the authors have used the process of writing to make sense of their experience. Teachers have told us that the struggle to put ideas and experiences on paper helps them to become clearer, more reflective practitioners. Under the right conditions, writing can be an occasion not only to reconstruct and revisit what has happened, but also to add new layers of meaning to experience.

For a long time, the idea of "teacher-proof" curriculum has captivated reformers who thought that learning and instruction would improve if outside experts researched and codified curriculum and pedagogy. The teacher, in a passive role, would simply implement what had been developed elsewhere. Lately this approach has given way to the idea of teachers as constructors of their own craft knowledge and designers of curriculum. This is a heartening development. In fact, no one can or should think for teachers. But what then is the role of another teacher's insights into teaching and learning if each of us must build his or her own knowledge about our craft? As Ron Berger, one of this book's contributors, has said about his own classroom, providing models of good work is an important way for people to learn from the experiences of others. Looking at the work of other teachers, reflecting on its qualities, and comparing it to one's own work are all ways we use to make sense of our own efforts and push our own practice further.

If the stories in this book are models or exemplars, what kind are they? They are, we hope, highly porous and nonprescriptive, written with an eye toward raising questions, provoking discussions, and stirring up thinking, rather than formulating an approach to be copied by others. A powerful story is one of the most convincing means we have as humans to convey the lessons of our experience. Though the stories in this book are, on the face of it, about craft and curriculum, we hope readers will look beyond their specific content to the larger issues and questions they point to.

Common Threads: A Curriculum Built on Exploration

An expedition is an apt metaphor for intellectual inquiry. A real-life expedition is a journey with a purpose. There is something intriguing and inviting, yet mysterious about the way it opens up before you; the deeper you are drawn into it, the more the terrain reveals itself. An expedition's mission is meaningful to expedition members because they must lend their hearts and minds to it. Through grappling with the problems, questions, and dilemmas that emerge along the way, they test their ideas and develop them further. When lost or confronted with an obstacle, expedition members have to acknowledge what they do not know without becoming paralyzed with fear. In finding their way through thorny problems and coping with uncertainty, expedition members make mistakes, ask questions, get help from each other, and acknowledge what do not know and what they have to do about it.

The remainder of this introduction highlights some of the key elements of an expeditionary curriculum. Although they share a common definition and vision, it is important to note that every author translates these into practice in his or her own way. That is how it should be. Only when teachers—whether in the solitude of their own classroom or in conversation with their colleagues—view this form of intellectual inquiry through their own practice will it hold any meaning.

Creating Strong Connections to the World Outside the Classroom

The authors of these stories grapple with how to bring the world into their classrooms and their classrooms into the world. We get a glimpse of classrooms that are not just places with four walls and desks, but include a variety of settings—inside and outside school—where children's learning takes place. When these teachers and their students take an excursion into the community, there is a strong sense of purpose behind it. Making a connection with the world—whether searching for artifacts, unearthing evidence, or conducting interviews—is not an end in itself, but a chance for children to pursue their ideas, questions, and passionately held interests, which they then bring back to their class for further study.

Ron Berger's story of a whole school expedition illustrates how much learning in school and learning out of school reinforce one another. Embedded in a larger expedition on the subject of water, students and faculty tested the water quality of the private wells in their rural community when residents become concerned about possible pollution. They learned techniques to measure lead and sodium pollution so they could assess the quality of the drinking water and the ecological effects of contamination. They drew on community experts and health officials. On a weekly basis the students held an assembly to give the school and community updates on the data collection and analysis. They provided frequent briefings for the town newspaper and health officials. It is readily apparent that an authentic, real-world problem drove this study.

Students used their field experiences to follow their hunches, gather data, observe phenomena, and interview experts. Back in class they analyzed what they had collected, reflected on what they had learned, and synthesized and presented their findings. While a study of water chemistry and ecology would have been possible without fieldwork, it would have been impoverished. Similarly, the fieldwork by itself, without the time for reflection that a classroom affords, might not have allowed students to deepen their thinking about what they uncovered.

Joining Relevance and Complexity

One of the many false dichotomies in educational discourse is the choice between making curriculum "relevant" to young people's lives—allowing it to "emerge" out of their ideas and concerns—and the belief that this approach is too narrow and is tantamount to subordinating the curriculum to children's prekindled interests (Brooks 1993). There is a way out of this conundrum through recognizing that learners' interests can be sparked by a great many subjects if one engages their intelligence and curiosity. It is true that childrens' ideas and understandings are often bounded by what they are ready to assimilate into their current views of the world. But the qualities of subject matter and how it is presented can strongly affect how well a learner intellectually takes hold of an idea. So, children's present understandings *are* the place to begin, but challenging content and teaching ("the right question at the right time") can nurture and accelerate their intellectual growth (Duckworth 1987).

Kathy Greeley's chapter "Making Theater, Making Sense and Making Change" describes her use of theater to engage students' ideas by placing the study of history and students' experiences together at the center of an expedition. As part of larger unit on change—How do societies change, and how do people change societies?—Greeley and her students examined the Holocaust and the Civil Rights movement as case studies of responses to intolerance, human degradation, and injustice. Greeley wanted her students to connect these epochal events to their lives. So, she and her students set about to write, produce, and perform a play that combined students' reflections on these historical events with their own experiences of intolerance. They looked at instances of heroism in their own lives— people they knew who had taken a stand against injustice and intolerance, and, closer to home, people who had shown responsibility by caring for their communities and families. This, Greeley writes, allowed students to "weave their lives closer to those of the people they were studying."

The authors in this book point to several characteristics of content that can kindle young people's curiosity and thinking. In general, such content builds on learners' current understandings; it encourages them to pursue their own questions and ideas; it engages their enthusiasm for learning; and it has a feel of authenticity. Lisa Schneier (1987) writes, "We sand away at the interesting edges of subject matter until it is so free from its natural complexities, so neat, that there is not a crevice left as an opening. All that is left is to hand it to them [learners], scrubbed and smooth, so they can view it as outsiders." Schneier's words urge us to respect and keep intact a subject's natural complexity, so the ambiguities and uncertainties are there to wrestle with. A subject matter that is rich with possibilities opens a great many pathways into it for different kinds of learners (Duckworth 1987).

Living in Trees

David Hawkins (1974), the educational philosopher, uses the metaphor of a tree to describe the learning that should lie at the heart of curriculum that fully engages a learner's intellect and imagination. Imagine yourself climbing a tree. At each branching limb you are faced with a choice or set of choices. You could go right or left, you could keep going straight, or you could turn around and go back the way you came, and so forth. After many such choices you begin to construct a history of the paths you have taken. The image of branches extending upward and forward underscores that we learn through our own initiative and activity. "The fruit that is found along the way is not merely consumed or assimilated; it is enjoyed as the fruit of active choice. What is laid down in memory is not merely the enjoyment, but the path that led to it," Hawkins writes. Hawkins contrasts this with another structure. If you follow a single branching pathway and cut off all the other branches you get a ladder. "Everything is now well-ordered. Of course not much fruit is left, and there are no choices. The ladder renders maps unnecessary, all you need is dutifully to follow your nose."

Several teachers in this volume describe expeditions that lend themselves to the image of branching trees. In allowing learners to pursue their ideas, questions, and puzzlements, these expeditions closely follow the contours of children's understandings, unfolding in a way that is respectful and attentive to children's own pacing.

On their first day of class, Steven Levy's students were confronted with an empty classroom and their yearlong assignment: to design and construct an ideal classroom. Their first task was to design and build a set of desks. As straightforward as this might seem, it immediately instigated other challenges. Would students each own their own materials, or would materials be owned by everyone? This led to discussions about the virtues of community property versus private ownership. They studied colonial history to uncover how the Pilgrims handled such dilemmas. When the class settled this issue, another problem came to the fore: How would they find the money to build the desks? Of the many ideas they explored, attracting local investors to back their scheme seemed like the best strategy. But to entice investors they would have to pay dividends, which meant making a profit. Along the way, the class consulted with financial experts to learn about investment practices such as drawing up contracts with their investors, marketing shares for their product, opening an interest-bearing savings account, and so forth. Each challenge the class faced, each decision they made, brought with it others that led them deeper into their project and the related content they were studying.

The high school students in the chapter "Where in the World Are We?" followed a similar path of inquiry, but with a very different kind of subject matter: the physics of locating an object in space. Instead of handing students contrived, polished experiments out of a textbook, the teachers encouraged students' questions about things they had a burning interest to know: If you are setting up a satellite dish in your backyard, and you want to receive a transmission from a satellite, how do you know where to find it in the sky so you can point your dish at it? And how do you point a satellite so it hits something here on earth? Or, how do you program a robot to move from one point in space to another? The teachers also presented the students with materials they could use to explore their questions—a preassembled robot arm, a solenoid, a parabola—and encouraged them to seek out experts in the community who could aid their investigations: a local manufacturer of robotics parts, a cable television station, an electrical engineer.

Real-world problems present themselves in exactly the way these students experienced them. There was no linear, cookbook-like set of steps to follow. Each decision presented a new choice or set of choices requiring fresh insight. The messiness and unpredictability of the problems allowed students to follow their own questions and ideas, deviating from their path of investigation if they thought it necessary, to retrace their steps or forge ahead on some new line of thinking.

"You Are Crew, Not Passengers"

Just as an expedition to a remote mountain range requires its members to prepare carefully and pool their efforts, many of these authors design curriculum that calls upon learners to collaborate intensely on a project in which they are all deeply invested. The students in these stories work toward shared goals and outcomes that can best be accomplished by drawing upon the talents, interests, and efforts of the entire group. The founder of Outward Bound, Kurt Hahn, keenly understood the educative power of small groups. He believed that communities are shaped through shared commitment. One of the key aims of schools, as Hahn saw it, was to "harmonize the social and intellectual differences between students by operating as a community of participation and active service" where students balance their own personal goals within a larger purpose (James 1995). "You are crew, not passengers," Hahn told the students at the school he established in Germany in 1920. Just as there are times during an expedition when each individual acts on his or her own personal initiative, so there are opportunities for students to place their formidable energies in service of the common good.

Both Greeley's and Berger's expeditions evolved around authentic, challenging problems that drew students and faculty together. In Greeley's case, the shared goal of writing and performing an original play inspired students' commitment to one another and the project. The task was meaningful to each student—the ideas and hard work of each person were behind it—while at the same time their goal was bigger than any one individual. Likewise, in Berger's expedition, the project had opportunities for adults and others to depend on the actions of young people to address a vital community issue. The children approached their work with great care and a collaborative spirit, nurtured in part by the message they received from teachers and other adults that their actions mattered, and that they could be trusted with important affairs.

In Susan McCray's story "Making the Circle Bigger" the tragic slaying of a young person and the feelings of anger and grief surrounding his death launched a student-led project to strengthen the school by encouraging young people to make a difference in their community. As a crew, the class set out to draw the school together through constructing a park on the theme of hope and unity. "Making the circle bigger," a theme that came from one of McCray's students, "became our mission; it was the vision that drove and united us," she writes.

In a wide range of ways, the metaphor of a crew is useful when thinking about the classroom—a whole class as well as smaller working groups. The following chapters illustrate a variety of groupings of students and roles for individual learners. For groups of students to become "crews," a teacher establishes clear structures and ground rules, and teaches cooperative skills. There is explicit attention to group process and to how people treat each other. A culture of sharing, collaborating, listening, constructive critique, and thoughtful discussion animates these classrooms. Mary Lynn Lewark writes about her first graders' peer critique sessions, "I feel okay about putting their work out there because we're close enough to handle it.

We are starting to create a language about how to give each other feedback. There's an important phrase in my class, 'Let's practice' . . . it's a space in which to try [out new ideas and work]."

Reflection and Assessment— Getting a Sense of Where You Are

No expedition sets out without a strong sense of where it is going, and without pausing along the way to take its bearings. But rarely do expedition members know the lay of the land they are about to explore before they embark, so they must build in frequent opportunities for self-correction and evaluation to determine and stay their course. The teachers in this volume nurture an ethos where reflection is the norm, and in which discussing, conferring, revising, and critiquing are common practice. There is explicit emphasis on effort, perseverance, and doing one's personal best. Through providing lots of opportunities for learners to take stock of where they stand in relation to clear standards, these teachers place success within students' reach.

The role of reflection in revision emerges strongly in these writings. In one case, Mary Lynn Lewark uses the idea of public versus private audiences with students to get across the importance of revising work with different readers in mind. When students put on a play at the end of the year, the point becomes still clearer. They come to see that "public work is like a performance, rehearsals are like rough drafts, and your final performance is where everything comes together. You need to know your lines. You have to know your steps." Lewark deepens her first graders' relationship to their writing by drawing on the experience of the play to reinforce the revision process. She does this by helping them to see their work through the eyes of different kinds of audiences. "I know you understand," Lewark tells her students, "but what are you going to do so I can understand, because you might not be there to explain [your work] to me?" Throughout the stories in this book, there are many other examples of how reflection can be used and framed to support the revision process.

For these teachers, reflection has everything to do with getting inside the minds of their students. By getting close to students' ideas, they find they have better information to guide their next steps. They also learn how children respond to various kinds of content, enabling them to structure better ways for children to take hold of subject matter. How do these teachers do this? They closely observe students at work on complex tasks and projects, ask them questions about what they are working on and thinking about, and pose questions that push their thinking a little further. The teachers are then better prepared to ask themselves, "What's worth having children struggle with? Is there adequate complexity here? Are learners that come in contact with this content faced with questions and puzzles of their own making? Do they find this subject matter intriguing and inviting? Do they have a sense that it leads somewhere?"

In "Window into Students' Thinking," Kathy Greeley writes about the importance of reflection for her own practice. At the outset of her experimentation with project-based work, she laments, "I didn't know what [students] were thinking. I didn't even know *if* they were thinking. How could I crack through this wall?" Greeley comes to find that students' project work provides the evidence she is looking for. Students' work, if it fully engages them, offers her valuable information that informs her decisions as a teacher. "I felt as if someone had suddenly cut a window into their heads, and I could get a glimpse into these students' thinking."

Throughout this book, teachers describe a wide variety of ways in which students reflect on the qualities of their work. Together students look at exemplars of good work, reflect on the elements of successful projects, and ask themselves questions such as "What do we value in good work?" and "How will we know we have done a good job?" From these discussions they generate criteria for excellence. Then students hold their own and others' work up against these standards. Criteria like these serve as "road maps for arriving at our goal of producing a high-quality product," writes Greeley. In "The World Is Mine. Soon. I Hope," Loretta Brady writes, "We need robust, honest dialogue around samples of real students' work so they can clearly see what good work looks like, and how to get there."

High Stakes and Standards

"Whenever I begin an expedition with my students I want them to feel it asks the impossible," Steven Levy has said. "I want them to believe that it can't be done. And then, somehow, we do it." The learning expeditions described here aim for heights that, at first glance, exceed what could reasonably be expected of students. Like history's great expeditions, these intellectual journeys start with difficult, seemingly unattainable goals and destinations, but ones that are worthy of students' best efforts. The arduous, complicated work that students undertake to achieve their goal lends it special meaning and significance.

The authors of the book offer several concrete but multidimensional ideas for enabling and inspiring students to achieve at high levels: classroom-based standard setting, teachers' ongoing reflection on their practice in light of students' work products, and public displays of student work.

The path to higher standards, some of these authors suggest, leads through a shared vision of what excellence looks like and "how to get there," to use Brady's words. These are not lifeless, rigid standards of what students should know and be able to do. Rather they come from classrooms and schools, like those described in these chapters, where students and teachers wrestle with what they mean by good work, and where the values they articulate are at the core of teaching and learning. They are dynamic, fluid standards that arise from conversations where students and teachers constantly negotiate, and revisit their meaning through looking and relooking at actual work. In classrooms like these, teachers ask themselves, "Do my students own the standards? Are they at the center of students' reflection and revision?" As Greeley writes about her play, "The class understood that getting responses, shaping, and reworking was the way to reach the standards we set for ourselves."

Getting standards out of the dark and into the open also helps teachers get clearer about good practice. When Brady and her colleagues held up their students' work against their standards, they "were forced to confront some shocking revelations. While we noted strong growth in almost all of our students, we were greatly disturbed by the discrepancy between our ideal standards (our middle school exit requirements) and the level of quality we observed in many of our students' work." When coupled with reflection, standards reach back into practice. Teachers are forced to ask themselves, "If our standards state what we would like students to know and be able to do, are we offering adequate opportunities for them to achieve at this level?"

One of the vehicles several of the authors in this book use to raise standards is performance and other public displays of student work. After students have engaged in an intensive process of examining models, developing criteria, and repeatedly revising their own work, a public exhibition is an opportunity to deepen learning. Getting student work out of the classroom and into the public domain has several effects. First, it raises students' investment. As Greeley writes, "This play was our creation. It expressed our inner thoughts and emotions. Other people were going to see it." And Lewark writes about wanting "to give them a history with what it's like to stand up in front of a group and put their work out there." When students know from the beginning of a project that they will share their work with a larger audience, they are often willing to engage in the demands of producing excellent work. Second, at times an audience can play a role providing useful critique, helping students to understand what needs to be done to reach high standards. Finally, a public performance also enriches the entire community's understanding of the qualities of good work; it moves a community—parents, students, school leadership, and teachers—closer to a vision of excellence by offering tangible evidence of students' learning.

Duehr and Flatt tell us in "Truck, Boat, Train, Bus" that they had grown accustomed to family nights with rows of chairs and a teacher-orchestrated student performance that involved more telling than showing, with parents in a passive role. But at the end of their expeditions, the teachers saw that the student project work spoke for itself; they did not have to reframe or interpret it for parents. What parents needed was to see and handle the work and discuss it with the children. "The quality of the work drove the chairs away," they write. "The walls were plastered with artwork and posters that demonstrate the progression from earlier drafts to final ones, which said so much more about revision than anything we could have told them." By engaging with the work, seeing its quality and variety, and talking with the children, parents gained a clear and grounded view of what the class was striving toward.

The stories in this collection point to truths about teaching and learning that have been known and embraced by many educators for generations. The notion of an intellectual expedition may be new and unfamiliar in the context of schools and classrooms, but the underlying principles are not. The following stories show us that curriculum can be both thoughtfully designed by teachers and open to students' choice and discovery; that it can address the major disciplines and essential skills as well as students' passions and interests; and that it can challenge both the mind and the heart.

■ ■ ■

Brooks, J.G. and Brooks, M.G. *The Case for Constructivist Classrooms.* Alexandria, Virginia: Association for Supervision and Curriculum Development, 1993.

Duckworth, Eleanor. *The Having of Wonderful Ideas and Other Essays on Teaching and Learning.* New York: Teachers College Press, 1987.

Hawkins, David. *The Informed Vision: Essays on Learning and Human Nature.* New York: Agathon Press, 1974.

James, Thomas. "The Only Mountain Worth Climbing: An Historical and Philosophical Exploration of Outward Bound and Its Link to Education." In *Fieldwork: An Expeditionary Learning Outward Bound Reader,* 57-70. Dubuque, Iowa: Kendall Hunt, 1995.

Schneier, Lisa. *Why Not Just Say It?* (Unpublished paper, Harvard Graduate School of Education, 1987).

About the Editors
and Contributors

Ron Berger teaches sixth grade at Shutesbury Elementary School in Shutesbury, Massachusetts. He also consults with Expeditionary Learning Outward Bound.

Loretta Brady is a middle school teacher at School for the Physical City in New York City.

Meg Campbell is executive director of Expeditionary Learning Outward Bound and co-director of the Harvard Outward Bound Project at the Harvard Graduate School of Education.

Emily Cousins is a writer and editor who has worked with Expeditionary Learning Outward Bound since its inception in 1992. She lives and works in Missoula, Montana.

Christine Cziko formerly taught high school humanities at School for the Physical City in New York City. She now teaches at Thurgood Marshall Academic High School in San Francisco, California, and chairs its English department.

Tammy Duehr is a first- and second-grade teacher at Table Mound Elementary School in Dubuque, Iowa.

Shari Flatt is a first- and second-grade teacher at Table Mound Elementary School in Dubuque, Iowa.

Kathy Greeley teaches seventh- and eighth-grade humanities at Graham and Parks School in Cambridge, Massachusetts. She also consults with Expeditionary Learning Outward Bound.

Donna Green is a computer science and math teacher at Deering High School in Portland, Maine.

Marie Keem was a research assistant with Performance Assessment Collaboratives for Education at Harvard University in Cambridge, Massachusetts. She also consulted with Expeditionary Learning Outward Bound. She presently lives and works in Paris, France.

Steven Levy teaches fourth grade at Bowman School in Lexington, Massachusetts. He also consults with Expeditionary Learning Outward Bound.

Mary Lynn Lewark teaches kindergarten, first- and second-grades at Rocky Mountain School of Expeditionary Learning in Denver, Colorado.

Susan McCray teaches seventh- and eighth-grade humanities at Graham and Parks School in Cambridge, Massachusetts. She also consults with Expeditionary Learning Outward Bound.

Amy Mednick is communications director with Expeditionary Learning Outward Bound.

Javier Mendez teaches middle school at Rafael Hernandez School in Boston.

Connie Russell-Rodriguez teaches middle school at Rafael Hernandez School in Boston.

Leah Rugen is associate director of Expeditionary Learning Outward Bound.

Vivian Stephens is a fourth-grade teacher at Clairemont Elementary School in Decatur, Georgia.

John Sweeney is a physics teacher at Deering High School in Portland, Maine.

Denis Udall is a researcher/school designer with Expeditionary Learning Outward Bound.

Larry Wheeler teaches math at Deering High School in Portland, Maine.

Dennie Palmer Wolf is executive director of Performance Assessment Collaboratives for Education at Harvard University.

1

"The World Is Mine. Soon. I Hope."
The Struggle to Raise Standards

Loretta Brady

Against the backdrop of a learning expedition on activism and community involvement called "Can We Change the World?" Loretta Brady writes about learning to teach to high standards in an urban school. She follows the struggles and triumphs of two middle school students as they come to see their work in light of their own heightened expectations for themselves and their project work. At first the students balk, even resent holding their work to higher standards. But as they delve into the qualities of their work products through ongoing revision and conversations with other students, their "images of excellence" become clearer and more personal. Brady, who teaches at School for the Physical City in New York, helps students make a link between reaching for higher standards in school and making a difference in the world around them. Through studying the lives of history's great leaders and activists, Brady's students come to expect more of themselves and gain a new appreciation of their role in making change.

> *My wire sculpture is a globe and*
> *resembles me because the world is*
> *mine. Soon. I hope.*
> Alfredo, seventh grade

Alfredo reads on a fourth-grade level, his test files announce. "Watch out or I'll snuff you," he warns, as if to say hello. He saunters by the school desks, shoulders dipping back and forth to unheard rhythms. The sheer mass of his thirteen-year-old body makes him a child-man, upper arms so round they barely rest against his body. Other days he moves his desk to the window, slumps passively, and stares ahead, sucking the baby blue plastic rosary beads that encircle his sturdy neck. Someday he wants to run his own business, Alfredo says.

1

Hannah's hair tangles about her face and sweeps down to her desk, hiding tiny hands that roll and remold her "squeegie," a lime green, polymorphous goop the texture of chicken gizzards. Her child-like ways belie mature, poetic genius. "My poems are dark and serious," Hannah reflects, "which is why I think they are good writing and that I'd be good for writing something important." Though a high scorer on standardized tests, Hannah broods bitterly when asked to free-write a page about any idea that has struck her during class discussion. Cats are the only subject she'll write about at length. Once she wrote about the way she likes to lie on her living room floor, cradling a little kitten on her stomach so she can feel its tiny bones tremble when it breathes.

In 1990 I left a job as a humanities instructor at a private secondary academy to carry the torch of high standards to the public domain. Alfredo and Hannah were among the kinds of students I longed to rescue: unconfident, resistant, low-achieving. I longed to fight in the battle for equity, longed to bring high expectations to a low-budget setting. What a bargain! And could I make demands! I was Mother Theresa with a perfection complex. It was exciting, romantic even. In police parlance, I wanted to be the first through the door. Sure, some students might take a few extra years to graduate, but they wouldn't mind when they saw the high standards they were achieving. Embraced by children of mixed gifts and backgrounds, placed in the arms of a loving school—its mission clear, its standards high—they couldn't help but succeed. Success was just a matter of time.

If I had only known then what I know now.

"I Don't Care. You Don't Scare Me, Lady."

I had no idea how emotionally painful the struggle for high standards would be. I first met Alfredo and Hannah in the opening year of the School for the Physical City (SPC), an Expeditionary Learning center focusing on New York City issues and leadership. A joint effort of public and private sectors, this public school was the lovechild of several parents: New York City Outward Bound; the prestigious Cooper Union; the Mission Society; and Expeditionary Learning Outward Bound.

In that first school year, a fifteen-year-old accidentally cut open a vein after hearing he had failed a course; he smashed his fist through a glass window. For Alfredo, the threat of high standards meant a vote with his feet. He wandered frequently to the frustrated learner's favorite resource, the bathroom. When confronted with demands for more effort and higher standards, he'd answer, "I don't care. You don't scare me, lady." It took Hannah a year to convert her hostile sarcasm into an articulate distaste for me and my standards. Responding to a set of self-reflection prompts for her reading portfolio, she wrote:

Dear Loretta,

"*Everyday I grow a little older, but I have to say that I'm not getting any better as a seminar reader or essay writer. It's the N's you always give me that cause me to think this way* ["Not yet meeting standards" or "Needs improvement"]. *You always tell me to do my work over again. Why can't I bring myself to even try to do it over again? Why do I get depressed just thinking about trying? The answer is that I don't even feel like it. Rewriting is a huge bummer. But you always keep on me until my essays are perfect. I've always known that group discussions weren't for me. People put me down. They don't take my comments seriously . . . I don't want to go any deeper into it. The memories are too painful. I know that this is the way seminars are suppose to be—everyone sharing and contributing—but can't you bend the rules for me?*"

Hannah

Failure hurts. It was sure killing me. All this time I had thought Hannah and Alfredo were learning strong skills and a can-do attitude from their peers. Instead, they suffered in silence. For them, and some others, our universally high expectations fueled anger and despair instead of confidence and hope.

The opening-year curriculum explored New York City's historic struggles with tolerance amid diversity. The irony wasn't lost on us. Naively, as a staff we had taken the plunge to establish a new breed of community where close human relations allowed a culture of critique to thrive, never fully grasping the challenging contradiction of being both supporter and judge. Although many students did experience success in moving toward higher standards, it was never an effortless victory. In hindsight, it's not surprising. Among entering students' estimations of what made good work: "When your work shows effort, you get an A"; "It has to be neat, with nice lettering"; "It's long."

Students have naturally built-in bullshit detectors. They are expert judges of the originality, realism, or practicality of an idea. Critique and revision were like muscles they hadn't been asked (or been interested enough) to use. Even students from so-called rigorous schools had vague notions about how to make reading responses more thoughtful, initially clutching their pages to their chests, defending: "These are my *feelings*. Waddya mean they're not good enough?" Sometimes parents hollered along.

Nonetheless, when we used descriptive criteria task checklists, strong exemplars of good and emerging work, and the rich evidence of portfolios, most conflicts yielded deeper growth. By the end of the first year, most students were sufficiently able to track their own progress toward meeting standards, especially textual analysis, which we agreed was the foundation for most conceptual learning. It really began to seem that our hunch was right. We believed that everyone has a natural desire to learn, and that, when properly tapped, everyone naturally desires quality too.

> *Before I came to this school, I never knew what a seminar was, or felt comfortable defending my opinions, never even heard of outlining, much less knew how to use one. Baby, look at me now. I give examples and counterexamples and I'm good at making connections between the ideas of writers. I know how to find strong evidence and quote writers. You can't shut me up. And I'm the first one to point out when someone's evidence is weak. Even though I forget and say things that can get a bit mean, I really do respect other people's ideas and the way they challenge mine.*

In some ways, we felt smug. While bureaucrats were making abstract lists of what students should know and be able to do and calling these curriculum frameworks "standards," we at least understood that far higher standards were achieved when the knowing is framed as a concrete task— a "performance"—that is personally meaningful and rich in the ideas at the heart of a discipline. The ideal task is not merely fun (a frequent misunderstanding), but purposeful and stimulating, allowing students to construct knowledge in ways that are meaningful for them. At best, our tasks asked students to apply disciplinary understandings, and then to present them clearly to a wider audience. Students responded well to our first-year tasks, which ranged from student-written plays to simulated policy debates to community oral histories and service projects.

Nevertheless, as we scrutinized our work among ourselves—for we teachers, as well, needed public space to present our standards—we were forced to confront some shocking revelations. Although we noted strong growth in almost all of our students, we were greatly disturbed by the discrepancy between our ideal standards (our graduation-from-middle-school exit requirements) and the level of quality we observed in many of our students. This was one of Alfredo's best pieces at the end of seventh grade:

Dear Bea and Arthur,

> *I liked when I went to visit you because I liked your company and I hope you liked my company, too. Thanks for sharing your stuffed*

cabbage. I learned you can do a lot of things with beans and yarn. How many people are in your family? See you next month.

Your friend,
Alfredo

Hannah wasn't much better off. Though she was a stunning painter and poet, there wasn't much else she would do. It wasn't good enough. We had to increase our demands and increase our support. We'd continue to support their passions, for it's nearly impossible to create quality unless we care about the creation. We'd give further support with booster reading and writing classes. But then came the harder question. As they struggled to master disciplinary concepts and skills, as they handed in assignments day after day, how far could we push them to add and revise? How good is good enough?

Mercifully, I was to instruct Hannah and Alfredo again the following year—my colleagues agree it takes at least two years for teachers and students really to know one another, to know what keeps them engaged in the struggle for quality work. I was eager to try again.

We had started our school without the images of Hannah and Alfredo before us. I hadn't known the boy whose bold commands would steady the rhythm of our wobbly canoe, the crew lurching through turbulent waters off Manhattan's northern coast during one of our first Outward Bound adventures. I hadn't known the twelve-year-old girl who would corner editorial control of our poetry magazine just so her verses earned prominent display.

I Love My Family, But They're In Trouble. They Need Support.

That was the phrase Alfredo painted on a schoolwide mural, a kick-off art project for a year's exploration on the problem of change, the essential generative theme for the integrated humanities program in our second year. Now, knowing the way he loved using his hands, loved messing about with cameras, computers, and stage sets, I especially had this eighth grader in mind while our team designed an entry-point miniproject.

We visited larger-than-life political murals painted boldly on colorful tenement walls throughout New York City's neighborhoods. Then we each created or selected a quote to paint on movable canvas panels, our collective artistic protest about something that mattered most to us, something we wanted changed. "My family needs help" was Alfredo's message, but he cringed at its connotations—too blunt, too pitiable, too cliché. He sensed it intuitively: people turn off when you show too much need. He struggled for expression, a way to be heard, learning crucial lessons about the precision of words. Not bad for a boy who never seemed to care about fragments, commas, or grammar.

Such tasks were good, but not good enough. Too often we forfeit the full power of teaching as we struggle to design engaging tasks. Too many middle schools overemphasize skill goals or quality in neatness and presentation. We perhaps fear that by building in required high standards for disciplinary understanding (especially for the thoughtful application of disciplinary knowledge) we will sacrifice the fun and engaging elements of a project. Afraid we'll face resistance or confuse learners, we underestimate our ability to design tasks that bring to life the very heart of our disciplines. Certainly it means more work, work I'd never try doing alone again.

Growing Together

All that second year we were probing the notion "Can we change the world?" I knew students had to feel first the power of their own personal, inner changes in order to construct full meaning from the stories of the lives of great grassroots and governmental activists. Then we could pursue our standards for excellence in analytic reading, writing, and research and in disciplinary understandings about the very engines that drive political change in a democracy.

A great breakthrough for Alfredo came with a task designed to link thematic and structural understandings of our literature to an autobiographical bookmaking project. (This was a project to which we'd return twice more that year as a way to give students more distinct references for tracking their own growth.)

One day, his mind empty of ideas about a story of change, or the motivation to find one, Alfredo was struck by a classmate's writing. One Christmas, this boy had been burned by a woodstove in his family's winter home, and now even on Outward Bound trips, he is still afraid of campfires. Then Alfredo shared *his* story. When he was four, one Sunday morning in his family's apartment, he had wanted to see some matches light up, and wound up setting the kitchen garbage pail on fire. His parents stuck his hand in the flames so he'd "never do that again."

The writing task was carefully designed for quality control. It stated the standards for excellence explicitly yet flexibly. Based on our close reading of many rich models, from writers as diverse as Piri Thomas, Marion Wright Edelman, and Mark Twain (Alfredo particularly enjoyed Twain, at least in an adapted version publishers sell as a "third-grade level" reading), the task asked students to "write about a time in your life when you changed, or when you hoped or feared something about you would change. You need to show two side-by-side narratives in enough detail to unfold your theme to the reader, considering all the same standards you pointed out and evaluated when we read adult writers."

I was afraid I was going to get hit some more [wrote Alfredo in his much-labored memoir, "The Boy Who Played with Fire"], *so I ran away down the hall past the scary statue of Papa Díos. I was afraid with those eyes he was about to punish me, too. Whenever my cousins slept over, we used to pretend it was a ghost. . . . Now, I'm scared of nobody. My parents will yell and punish me when I break curfew. My mom's eyes bug out. She screams and cries. But I'm not scared. Still, I can't look in her eyes . . .*

Up until that point, many of the others had been writing skinned-knee stories, more plot than reflection. Alfredo made it cool to open up. Later on, when Alfredo found out I'd put copies of his memoir in each teacher's mailbox—that *he* was now the school exemplar—he polled the staff for feedback. Now when adults see him wandering the halls, he's often looking for someone to read drafts of his essays. He craves readers. His revision wasn't automatic, or entirely fun, but he had concrete images of what excellence meant, and a personal reason, his book, why quality mattered.

Still, despite such vivid experiences, the institutional culture clung tenaciously to most students. Making transitions is difficult. We asked what SPC high school students would be like, what evidence in their work would show that they had moved beyond middle school standards. Most of them felt, "Hey, you have to pass your classes." Once, in a fitful reaction after I wouldn't accept poor-quality homework, Alfredo sneered, "You're making this a school for the gifted," as though high-quality work were genetically linked. It would take some time before they—and we—understood the cumulative picture of what we were trying to achieve. In the meantime, we had to build a buzz, make it exciting—with magazines, contests, and so forth.

But even more, they needed to construct their own understanding of the whys and hows of quality if we wished the culture of high standards to stick. A pivotal step in that direction was our collaborative evolution of standards.

Together we designed a simple continuum for a good reading group leader, for a strong reading log, for an excellent seminar essay. We tested these out with student samples from schools far and wide, then students ranked themselves along their own continuum. It helped to keep the stakes low; we still had weeks before interim report cards, plenty of time to move ourselves along on the spectrum. Ironically, Alfredo and Hannah were the harshest critics. Go figure.

Alfredo's anger over having booster reading classes instead of more art time was somewhat appeased as he came to understand his own growth as a reader. In our reading portfolio we hope for a rich array of evidence, from standardized tests to student-generated vocabulary words, questions, annotated "marked-up" text pages, log responses and notes on themes and textual analyses; notes from skits, trials, and discussion leading; and essays defending an idea with the use of textual evidence. By the middle of the year, Alfredo knew he had far to go, but he was able to acknowledge concrete ways in which he had seen growth, as well as steps he could take himself.

> *I am reading more now. The strategies that help me best are when Evan reads to me, especially about facts. When I read them by myself, they get boring. But not when he reads them. It helps me ask more questions and I think about other books I know about. I also finish more books and harder books by myself. Before, even small words were hard for me, but now I read bigger words and longer books. I need to stay more focused and keep doing my work.*

The extent to which a student himself can articulate increased expectations, I'm now convinced, is the extent to which he starts to reach them. Above all, I'm fully persuaded that it is Expeditionary Learning's ten principles that provide a sturdy infrastructure, the safe, supportive framework that allows us to challenge individuals to their highest potential. It's a bit too easy to mock. Adventure education? Is that when troubled teens and new age corporate execs blindfold their partners for a trust walk over to hug their favorite tree? Yet Expeditionary Learning asks us to test ourselves, explore our inner boundaries. That's adventurous education.

"All students must be assured a fair measure of success in learning to gain confidence," the design principles read, ". . . but it is also important to experience failure, to prevail against adversity." Though we hate to face it, mistakes are human, and plentiful, but are in fact opportunities as well. Expeditionary Learning challenges schools to find tasks with an inherent real-world challenge, tasks whose purpose and consequences really matter for some other people. Just as Outward Bound sets up real consequences for not mastering skills—if you don't know what you're doing, you'll put your partner on the rock face at risk—there are ways to structure learning projects that maximize an inherent need to master excellent skills, a need to know more. It's not unlike exhibition performances, but with a higher octane rating. In exhibitions, quality is a matter of personal responsibility and pride. In expeditions, quality is a quest, both personally and, more significantly, as a community.

Can We Change the World?

"Shut up! Why you make that face for, huh?" Alfredo shouts down a new girl in the class; the room is silent. I had just asked who'd like to join the next small group visiting the AIDS nursery when the new girl curled her lip. She had joined the class just a few weeks earlier. She didn't know the great passion with which our class members protected their activist service projects, Hannah and Alfredo in particular.

Alfredo and his classmates lifted toddlers high to let them score baskets, while Hannah and other students improvised a puppet show that ended when students gave an invitation: "Okay, if you want to see the puppet turn back from a potato into a little boy, clap your hands. Come on, clap louder, louder." The new girl knew nothing about this, knew nothing of those magical moments, a point of no return for that group of teenagers. "Those little guys are crazy," Alfredo laughed when six three-year-olds jumped his back and poked his rounded belly at a Head Start center they also visited. Our crew of twenty had done something extraordinary, and we'd never be the same as a group again.

Employing expeditionary frameworks and attitudes, our curriculum was designed so students would construct their own understanding of what it means to make a difference in one's community though their own experience of working with community activists in grassroots human service organizations. Similarly, they were to face "solo" expeditions that would apply their new skills and disciplinary understandings of the history of American government and leadership for change—through judicial, legislative, and executive powers. This was the guts of democracy. Most learning came through lively reenactments, judicial review, and in-depth Socratic seminars about the big ideas and great texts, among them, our nation's founding documents. In a pre-unit brainstorming of what they knew and wanted to know about community activism and change, Alfredo and his classmates were amazed to realize how many activists they already knew. They were also curious: *Why* was activism so often fatal? And if people failed in reaching their goals, they wanted to know, could you still consider them activists?

I remember clearly that day when the new girl fatefully rolled her eyes as this crew planned their next visit. An outsider to their experiences, she could not be expected to understand, try as they might to explain. The ensuing discussion evolved from her defense. She had a problem helping people who, she felt, should do more for themselves. If you helped people too much, she reasoned, they got lazy.

"Whaddya mean? You mean like this school helps you," someone asked, "but we should stop because it might make you get lazy?"

"No, that's not a good example," she said, "because this is a school. It isn't the real world."

"Whoa, lady," Alfredo called. "You mean this ain't the real world? Well, then, what is it, I'd like to know?"

I helped Alfredo negotiate a useful research topic. I designed the research task so students would write about a problem cities faced in the 1960s which we are still dealing with today. Students were to weigh these solutions and propose effective solutions for the 1990s. They had to discuss actual quotes, the very words of the activists themselves, as criteria for excellence in analytic research. They researched racism in Crown Heights, economic injustice for women, and even the inequity in public education. Throughout the research steps, we struggled to find primary sources Alfredo could read, guest speakers he could interview. Of all the final papers, Alfredo's was among the most carefully focused in understanding the problem/solution structure. "I am going to tell you about a few riots I studied that happened in L.A.," he wrote for this, his "solo" expedition, "the things that are the same, and the things that are different." "There are three things that might have prevented the latest riots, and future riots," Alfredo's proposal explained.

Hannah and Alfredo knew their service really mattered to those children. Similarly, they knew their proposals for change would be in the spotlight for our Activist Awards Night, an event that capped the end of the semester's projects. This celebratory "exhibition" lent a larger purpose and audience for their good work.

Raising the Bar

In the project where he lives, Alfredo is isolated, cut off economically and socially from mainstream culture. Here at his school, he belongs to a larger universe, a stronger community, and he knows it. There are those who believe Alfredo's isolation isn't the problem; the problem is Alfredo. They fear he drains school resources and dilutes school standards. To a big city bureaucracy, he is a pothole we can't afford to "fix."

We are at a pivotal moment in national reform. The stakes are high to see which forces control the direction of systemic change. In a setting of limited resources, policy makers everywhere are shaping decisions about which students are educable, and which are not.

I once worked at another new school, coaching diverse learners toward the habits of the life of the mind. After three years, certain students demonstrated very little mastery of the exit skills and understandings required to graduate. The staff made a decision: Begin a policy of competitive admissions. And I made a decision: Bail out.

Yet I struggled with the question of how accessible and fair some of our standards were, given the years of neglectful education many students had experienced. To permit diverse standards set off alarms in my head. I could not score Hannah's poems, however passionate, for their statistical analysis of the economic plight of women. Some modes of expression are simply not valid instruments for measuring all goals. At the same time, the better I understood the components of analytic research, the more open-ended the presentation could be: panel, trial, or debate. But a collage is not a research essay, a separate issue from the learning styles or multiple intelligences a child possesses. Furthermore, I still clung to the notion that becoming a good writer means becoming a better thinker. I wasn't ready to back off on standards for substantive writing.

I sought stories from everyone I could and got two kinds of advice. On the right, I heard voices counseling responsibility and imposed consequences. Students should "just do it." Human nature is lazy, yet nothing becomes easier without hard work, regular habits, practice. No pain, no gain. On the left, voices cautioned patience and encouragement. Don't worry, only engage. Keep doing personal writing until they are ready. Have them critique each other's work; don't impose your standards. Once young people are confident, they'll ask to do higher-quality work.

I sensed limitations in both lines of thought. The world seemed too complex for any one model. Furthermore, with so much recent excellent work from teachers in the area of standards and assessment, there were surely more tools at hand to bridge less confident learners toward a culture of higher expectations.

So at SPC a first step was to break the news lovingly that some students were in danger of not succeeding in entering into high school. We knew that they all could do it, and we were ready to prove it to them. But first, they had to carry their own backpacks up the mountain, or there'd be no dinner. Therefore, until their work habits, skills, and understandings reached stronger levels, we would impose mandatory afterschool tutorials. We prepared ourselves for resentment.

Scaling Walls

"Everybody says I'm just like Holden Caulfield. That's probably why I write like him, too." Hannah's reaction to mandatory tutorials was dramatic. For most of the students, the lunchtime study room had the feel of a picnic at a family reunion. Sitting alongside or bending over a student's desk were my colleagues, flooding the room with warmth and support. Not for Hannah. She moved her desk apart from the others, a book of Shakespeare's monologues propped open as her partition. Her whole stance announced, "I don't belong here with these kids!" Hannah would not carry her own knapsack. She had a special tutor for a learning disability (a tutor unwilling or unable to understand our standards), but Hannah insisted she needed no help.

In the first semester of eighth grade, Hannah's portfolio recorded mixed progress: elaborately drawn Venn diagrams as comparison outlines (but no written essay), attacks on Richard Wright's sexism when the class discussed his autobiography, and seminar texts highlighted with highly charged marginal asides. The few completed assignments she handed in missed the flavor of her oral brilliance—that is, when she was in the mood to speak up. Even with *Black Boy*—a novel she loved—where I allowed students a choice of challenges in deciding which chapters to read and present, she'd opt for the "novice" assignments, and even then leave the job half done. Sometimes she wrote summaries about the books she had finished for monthly independent reading assignments, fantasy adventure stories by Piers Anthony or other writers. It seemed that for years Hannah's verbal quickness had let her get away with murder—her own. Now, she lacked the habits, the confidence, and the skills to get the grades to which she'd grown accustomed.

"They want the Polo jacket at K-mart prices," my friend consoled me. "It's part of the culture. All you need is a dollar and a dream." That seemed as true about school reform as it was about grade-grubbing teens. We want quick answers at bargain prices. Whenever I returned papers to Hannah, it didn't matter how many facets of her work I praised; she focused on the grade, "Not meeting standards." Our report cards were mostly descriptive narratives of each child's strengths and weaknesses, and we kept portfolios to collect evidence of growth in reading and in communication of ideas. Although we never gave a cumulative grade, I still felt it important to state explicitly where their assessment projects stood against our standards: Does the work satisfy (S) or exceed (E) high standards? Or, does the work's emerging excellence need improvement (N) before reaching high standards? The system seemed the foolproof way to de-emphasize teacher judgment and transition students into a culture of internalized standards. But for Hannah it was a mountain she couldn't, or wouldn't, climb.

Don't let it bother you, I'd tell myself. But it did. Hannah had an acid wit, and I was often its target. Sorting and selecting their best work from their portfolios one day, I asked the students to place Post-it notes saying "Once Best" or "Burn This" on a piece they had earlier thought was excellent work, now that they realized their current progress. Hannah put one of the stickers on me. Ironically, we both deeply felt the pain of her failure—our failure. Perhaps the shame of mutual failure distanced us further, the way a couple's infertility might drive them apart.

Stewing, I began recalling something about Hannah at the end of that first semester. Even though she hadn't finished any research paper or written any speech, she showed up early at the theater for our Activist Awards Night dressed in a purple velvet jumpsuit with a French ruffled blouse. She kept sensuously brushing her long—usually windswept—hair; I think she even wore makeup. Trying hard to appear sophisticated, she was just a bit off, looking more like a schoolgirl in her best holiday outfit. I asked her if she wanted me to find something for her to read, but she declined. Then, in the midst of helping hang posters, she clutched my arm, saying, "Loretta, Loretta, what's the name of that poem that goes . . ." and proceeded to recite by heart an entire lyric of New York City's former resident poet Langston Hughes. "It came to me just now!" she said excitedly.

That night, in front of hundreds of people, unrehearsed, Hannah recited that poem, staring down at the stage floor as if the words were written there.

Suddenly, it all became clear. The outfit. The Shakespeare. The fantasy books. There was a performer as well as a poet in Hannah that was trying to get out. I went to her the next day for a talk. I told her how much I admired her quick, verbal strengths and her poetic genius. I explained that, to my mind, I felt I'd be cheating her if I didn't insist she learn to *write* persuasively, as well. Writing helps us think better, I told her. But more than that, the sexist economic injustice we both despised affects women sooner if they lack strong communication skills (as the job descriptions read).

With a bit of negotiation, we decided on two things. Instead of getting "Ns," she could work with me or another adult and get a grade of "S+ some help with . . ." That way we'd both recognize real growth, but she need never be frustrated again by an irrational fear of Ns. Furthermore, we came up with an idea whereby she could tape-record her essay along with songs from *Les Miserables*, one of her favorite stage experiences, as a comparison essay on the American and French revolutions. Later, a classmate or I could help transcribe, and she could revise. She liked the idea that she'd be taping music along with words; that way she'd feel more like a drama critic, she said, than a loser.

Hannah's energy focused as she gained more confidence—now attacking texts, not people. In one Socratic seminar, reading an excerpt of John Locke's definition of government (this was a unit on conflict and change in history), Hannah struggled together with her group to come to textually based understandings to such questions as: What is liberty, according to Locke? According to you? How does Locke believe power and authority differ? What are Locke's assumptions about people? Do you agree?

She particularly caught on to a thinking skill called doubting and believing, offering examples and counterexamples on her definition of liberty. "Wait," she asked the class, "isn't it true that power corrupts, but authority doesn't? How has that been true in our own government?" Our little performer was becoming a teacher. Possessed of a new freedom, she allowed herself to excel.

In her reading group, it was the same. Everyone else was stumped by this question: Do you think the author is pro- or anti-war, or both? Since the book was historical fiction, based on actual events and primary sources, they hadn't thought the author could shape a bias while he retold the story. But Hannah understood and pointed out passages where she could make inferences.

We sometimes create mini proficiency-based reading groups like this one that dissolve within a few weeks, providing yet another chance for students to select their own level of challenge and to accelerate or build stronger skills. Hannah chose but resented her "dumb" group until I proved to them their work was challenging too: I asked them to lead the sixth graders on a tour of New York City's Constitutional Heritage Trail, acting as actual literary or historical figures, but telling their interpretation of the conflict for self-determination.

Hannah went all out. She begged me to stay at lunch and go over her notecards with her. Dressed in a white colonial bonnet and holding a quill pen, she explained to the eleven-year-olds why she favored this new democracy, though she—who merely tended the tables in the tap room at Fraunces Tavern—was not yet allowed to vote. "Now ask me questions. Did you know I met Washington here? Did you know there was a murder mystery right here in this building, and here are the clues . . .."

While she continued struggling with essay forms, Hannah flourished with piles of new evidence of her development. We had the best of both: flexible, multiple forms to assess her growing use of textual evidence, and an unwavering eye as she continued struggling with the high expectations of the essay form.

The miraculous day ended with a scavenger hunt to find two war memorials nearby in that part of the city. Hannah had written out clues in lemon juice, the way the war spies had done in her novel. By the time we arrived at the memorial, a striking glass wall etched with letters from Vietnam veterans, we all felt as though we'd reached a mountaintop.

The next day Hannah requested a class meeting to tell the other reading group about their success. "We gotta show you those letters," Hannah told the class, "and the glass wall you can walk through and inside." Hannah and I worked it out so this next visit to the wall memorials would include the writing journal entries in order to compare the very different sculptural themes reflected in the two installations. We also planned a group initiative to symbolize the fact that we all need others to help us get over our individual walls, especially the walls that stand for our struggle to produce quality work.

The class was sold. Walls. What an apt metaphor it had become for Hannah.

These are two of the children who will be embraced or excluded in the new move toward raising national standards. Intense expectations require intense support. In a time of limited human and financial resources, support goes, more and more, to those seemingly motivated for high achievement. It's assumed too quickly that a student rejects high standards when what she's really feeling is frustration and despair. Students are written off too early.

We need more stories of students, of their struggles and our support. We need robust, honest dialogue around samples of real students' work so students can clearly see what good work looks like, and how to get there. The resources this will take are enormous—and not just for more staff, but most of all for more time, more time to plan, revise, monitor, and reflect. More time to teach and learn from students. The cost will be high; whether or not it's too exorbitant a price depends on your understanding of the accomplishment. Economics is only one kind of urban impoverishment.

Alfredo and I were sitting on a grassy plain, the great valley below. We were there reenacting the struggles of the American Revolution "on location." I asked if he could read his journal entry to the group, but he declined, explaining it wasn't "good enough."

With prodding, he did agree.

> *The mountains are beautiful, but they are the last I'll see. I have no shoes and my feet are bleeding. I have just seen my close friend die right next to me here. A bullet has got me now. I will never see you again, my family. The smoke and fog surround us. It's now quiet as a battlefield after the last bullet is heard. It's silent like death.*

Alfredo is in special education. Ours.

2

Let's Practice: Revision in a First-Grade Classroom

Mary Lynn Lewark with Denis Udall

In this chapter, first-grade teacher Mary Lynn Lewark describes an expedition in which her students study nutrition, cooking, weather, camping skills, and book publishing to create camping manuals for their own use. She also discusses strategies to help her students revise their projects through reflecting on the attributes of good work and the differences between producing work for public and private audiences.

Ground School[1]

As members of the kindergarten-second-grade team, we began the year knowing we wanted to design an expedition that involved a product the students would actually use. We also knew we wanted our students to prepare for an upcoming camping trip. That is how we came up with the project—a camping manual. The manuals are intended for a kindergarten or first-grade class at my school, the Rocky Mountain School of Expeditionary Learning in Denver, Colorado, or another Expeditionary Learning school.

First, I broke my students up into teams. Each team had responsibility for creating its own manual, and each team member wrote his or her own chapter. This helped to address a concern that parents have voiced: "I know these projects are supposed to be collaborative, but I need to see my child's work." There was a chapter devoted to setting up the tent. Another de-

---

[1]"Ground school" is a term that teachers from the Rocky Mountain School of Expeditionary Learning (RMSEL) have borrowed from the world of technical rock climbing. Prior to ascending a rock face, a novice climber is instructed by a guide in the technical know-how they need to safely manage themselves and secure the lifeline of their fellow climbers. RMSEL's teachers and students use this metaphor to describe the early phase of a learning expedition when students become acquainted with the skills, collaborative learning strategies, and background knowledge necessary to launch into the heart of an expedition.

scribed the menu and how to prepare the meals. A third contained a list of the clothes and other gear the students had to bring, and so forth.

One child's mother was an artist and author. She came to talk to us about how books are made—a graphic artist does the paste-up, an editor works on the text, and so forth. The children began using that language. This parent also made a large book to hold the children's manuals. There was a table of contents and a pocket for each child's chapter. The children could remove the chapters and take them home or put them in their portfolios. This has helped the students to understand that they can have their own work but that it can also be part of a larger whole; they can take the work out and show it to others but still put it back.

We started by brainstorming a list of clothes we would need for the trip. But the students quickly saw that our choice of clothes depended on the weather. So we began following and graphing the weather reports in the newspaper and the daily fluctuations in temperature. We drew a picture of a person on a huge piece of paper and "dressed him up" in paper clothes that the children thought they would need for the coldest day.

Next we tackled the menu. I brought in a box of Sugar Pops, which they said they wanted to take, and a box of sugarless cereal. We figured out how much sugar was in each type. Eventually we decided that we would bring only cereal that had fewer than six grams of sugar per box. One of our mothers heard about this discussion, and told me she owned a health food store and would be willing to come in and talk to my students. She brought a food pyramid chart and talked about the need to "eat five to stay alive." The students really caught on to that. She took each team to the store, and they ate vegetable pasta with organic sauce and rice and beans—really healthy food. We made a group decision to have oatmeal for breakfast because the mother told us she would donate it. So we went from Sugar Pops to organic oatmeal!

The children who were responsible for deciding what we would eat had to write directions for preparing each meal. In order to model what it takes to do things step by step, I brought in popcorn, bread, peanut butter and jelly, and Kool-Aid. The teams figured out how to prepare each food and wrote up the steps, from plugging in the toaster to selecting the correct size bowl.

We also set up tents on the school grounds. One student from each team observed from the side and wrote up the steps involved in setting up the frame and covering it with a rain fly. So one manual reads, "Get out the tent. Put the star in position. Get the star ends" (the student's word for the piece that connects the rods). And then, "Snap star ends together."

The Trip

The day we took the bus to the mountains I had the students unpack their bags in the gym, and they worked with partners, checking off their belongings using their clothes and supplies manual. One partner would hold up a flashlight and the other would say, "Check," and mark it off her list. There was a lot of confusion. Everyone kept saying, "What's this say? I don't understand!" They couldn't read each other's writing or understand the drawings.

A father who is very new to the school came along to help out. The first night he couldn't get the children to work together. They were goofing off, and he came to me and said, "Mary Lynn, they're not going to get it together to prepare the food." And I said, "Well, I guess they're not going to eat." He said, "Can we do that?" I replied, "Well, I'm not going to make their dinner for them!" He looked at me as if to say, "I can't believe she's going to do this." But pretty soon the students came around to realizing that they would have to cook if they were going to eat.

What usually happens in these situations is that we as teachers say we're going to let the students do it on their own but then we end up doing it for them. As a teacher, I'm always asking myself, "Am I doing something that my students could be doing for themselves?" My answer to this question is always balanced with my learning goals. I try to be strategic about it. There are times when I prefer to do some of the work for my students. For instance, it might be better for me to find the library books for a project, because to teach them how to find the books at this point would distract us from the task at hand. We can always go back another time to learn those skills.

Back in School: Authentic Assessment at Work

What Makes a Good Manual?

Until we left, all the students were fine-tuning their manuals—making sure they had all the necessary information. During the trip they used each other's manuals, so they knew what worked and what did not. When we returned I spread the manuals out on the floor and asked, "What kind of problems did you run into? What do you think makes a good manual? What do you think they ought to look like when they're done?" The students had different answers: "We had a hard time using them because we didn't understand the pictures. They're too small"; "I couldn't read your handwriting"; "We need to have our words spelled right because we couldn't read anybody's writing"; and "You need big pictures in case a kindergartner can't read the letters." They also thought drawings should match the words, and that the drawings should be able to stand on their own because some children might not yet be able to read and would have to rely on the drawings.

One child's early draft of a menu displayed the meals in a way that was hard for the reader to understand. Lunch was in one corner, breakfast in another. To the viewer's eye there was no rhyme or reason. But through revising the child began to see that if you want people to be able to understand your manual, you have to put it in some kind of order. The children began experimenting with different ways of organizing their information. For instance, information in one manual was presented in two ways. The dates of the meals were ordered from left to right, and breakfast for the day was on the top of the first page, with dinner on the bottom. Ingredients were on one page, preparation was on another, and so forth. A second manual had two parts. The first part was devoted to "everything you need to know before you get started." The second part was concerned with how to make the meal.

When they began working out the bugs in their earlier drafts, the students spent a lot of time looking up words in the dictionary. One day we sat down to write, and I heard the children say, "I don't know how to spell this. I don't know what to do. How do you spell this?" They were getting stuck on spelling every word correctly rather than focusing on the content. Until this point they had written only first drafts. I had focused primarily on writing and not on mechanics. But then they became intensely interested in words and in knowing where to go to learn how to spell them correctly. I've tried to communicate to the children that there is a time and place for spelling correctly, but that they have to preserve their creativity. As a first-grade teacher, I'm at the beginning. I get to see where good habits begin and where they die. I like children to be purposeful, but I also want them to be relaxed about their work. The revision process can become overwhelming for children if they are not given time to enter into it. You have to give them time to do quality work. I try to raise the standards while also providing supports—in this case, in the form of ample time.

Everything I get now has a couple of drafts with it. We will be conducting a "math investigation" and I will get two or three drafts, even though I never asked for them. I like the fact that this comes from the students. They are beginning to understand that coming up with a quality product means taking your time, and being careful and thoughtful about it.

I've been talking to my children about re-reading their own and each other's work. It helps them to read another child's work to gain insight into their own. My children used to say, "I'm finished." They would write something and put it away. Lately I've been saying to them, "Has someone read it yet?" They ask someone to read it, but their reader often doesn't know what to look for. So I've begun encouraging them to come up with questions to ask when looking at each other's work.

Let's Practice

When we looked at our earlier drafts, it was hard for the authors who were being critiqued because children at this age have not had much experience with critiquing. What is nice about our class is that we have been together for over a year. So I feel okay about putting their work out there because as a group we are close enough to be able to handle constructive criticism. We are starting to create a language about how to give each other feedback. We don't say, "Your drawings are junk." There is an important phrase in my class: "Let's practice." I say, "Let's pretend that you're reading Josie's manual and you notice she doesn't have any drawings. What are you going to say to her? And how are you going to make sure you won't hurt her feelings?" So we practice how we're going to talk to each other. Now they say, "Well, I saw you don't have any drawings and I think they would really make your manual better."

When we say "practice," we know we will have another shot at it. We are not looking for the best right now. It means "Let's just try it." It's like saying, "Let's practice because this is something that we're going to value. Let's practice so that we can get good at it, and remember how to do it." It's not practice for practice's sake. It's a space in which to try. This language works for these children. We have a history with it.

Keeping Track

The students are learning how important it is to keep track of their drafts. It's like holding yourself accountable; it's evidence of your thinking. The students have to remember where their work is—finding it in the space, remembering and retrieving it. It's about learning to collect your work, so you can refer to it when you're revising. It's a lesson about responsibility—about valuing, and collecting your work. So we practice keeping track. I'll say, "Let's get your chapters together. Let's put them back in your books."

Public and Private

Christine Cziko (one of this book's contributors) has helped me put a name to something I have been struggling with. She talked about public versus private writing. Her insight came to me at a time when I had been trying to help my children understand what a portfolio is all about. And I found the distinction between public and private extremely helpful in explaining for what audience a portfolio is intended. The word public has a whole set of meanings attached to it. I have had many conversations with my children about what good writing is, but it's different to say, "You're going to produce a piece that other people will read. What do you think writing for the public means?" That little word is changing the way my children see things.

The children said that private writing is like what you put in your diary. You don't have to worry about spelling, the kind of paper you use, or whether it makes sense to other people. On the other hand, they felt that these things really do matter with public writing. One child made the analogy to being at home with your family—your room can be a mess, you might be wearing grubby clothes. But when company comes over, everything gets put away and you clean up. They also talked about public swimming pools and public libraries, and how they are open and accessible to the world.

So we're beginning to talk about what's different when someone other than yourself reads your work. I tell my students, "I know that you understand, but what are you going to do so that I can understand, because you might not be there to explain it to me."

It's interesting how this public/private discussion has influenced other aspects of their work. We had a conversation about selecting a single unit of measurement for determining how far we jump. If one person uses drumsticks to measure and another uses unifix cubes, how would we be able to compare?

Usually when the children wrote up their investigations, they would note, "He jumped five and a half." But five and a half of what, right? This time they included a description of how we decided to use drumsticks to measure, to jump from the same line, and to measure from the tips of our toes. The children wrote about their thinking so that they would remember and could tell others about it.

I had the children poll each other and graph the results to find out what unit of measurement we would agree to use. But some children fudged it a bit because they really wanted to use their own unit and not someone else's. Other children counted the same person twice or didn't count one or two students at all. Few children had a system for keeping track. This led to an interesting conversation when everyone came up with very different results using the same data source! So I had to say, "Where's your proof? You have to be able to back up your finding that the majority of children want to use drumsticks. You must present your data in a public form that will prove to others that you've done your investigation accurately."

There were other ways our public/private conversation has helped. In the past, while going through their math work folders, the children would come across a piece of their work and say, "What's this? I don't remember why I did this." For instance, they might have the computations of a math word problem, but would be unable to recall the problem itself. Or they might have gathered data and created a table, but couldn't remember what their investigation was about. So they had no way of choosing pieces for their math portfolio because they couldn't remember their intended purpose. Now, they have become much more aware about keeping track, not only for themselves, but also so that they can explain their work to others who weren't there at the time.

The students are beginning to see that public work is like a performance. We're preparing to end the year with an exhibition. They understand about practicing and getting it right when there's a physical dimension—for instance, staging a performance, or learning how to put on a climbing harness or tie a bowline so they can go on the ropes course. We talked about how rehearsals are like rough drafts—your final performance is where everything should come together. You need to have your costume. You need to know your lines. You have to know your steps . . . They're beginning to see all these parallels now that we're working on a performance of our own.

At the exhibition, the children will put their work on display and they will talk about it. They will have to do a lot of preparation. They will have to think about what they're going to say. They will have to practice it. They have had a history with researching, revising, and gathering information. And now I want to give them a history with what it's like to stand up in front of a group and put their work out there.

For the Next Time

Looking Back with New Eyes

What I loved about the camping expedition was that it was very clear. There was a beginning, middle, and end. The expedition was built around the pursuit of the work itself—producing a manual, and what it means to create something through multiple revisions. From the outset, the children knew there was going to be a final product at the end. Overall, it was extremely tight.

I'm only now beginning to see how clear the structure of the camping expedition was. It's only by looking at it through the lens of the expedition we're in the middle of now—the human body expedition—that I'm able to reflect on it. I didn't reflect much at the end of the camping expedition, but I think that's key. I wish I had looked back and thought about why it worked, and then built those pieces into this new expedition. For starters, creating the camping manual moved us through the content. But the current expedition doesn't have a tight vehicle that is taking us through it. It's just a lot of activities and experiments.

Also, the human body expedition has too many parts to it, and I'm not really sure how they fit together. The content is huge. The big questions have been, "What makes me alive? How do my body parts work together?" And then we broke the content into smaller units: "We breathe and pulse. We eat and grow. We stand and move. We think and feel." I'm frustrated because I feel the current expedition ran away from us. We're drowning in content. Content should be part of an expedition, but it should be driven by a project (such as the camping manual) or a performance that allows students to demonstrate what they know.

In hindsight I realize that I should have organized this current expedition around creating an anatomy book. It would have made so much sense to my children to adapt the structure we used in creating a camping manual to writing an anatomy book. One group of students might have researched the digestive system, another the skeletal system, a third, the circulatory system, and so forth. The students would have used the revision process. This would have reinforced the skills they learned in the earlier expedition. We could have continued the conversation about revision and why it's important. They would have had a public piece to share with others. As with the camping manual, the final product would have taken us through the expedition.

Teaming with Other Teachers

I have been thinking about teaming and how our kindergarten–second-grade team works together. We need to get better at making midcourse corrections, and not limiting our ideas about teaming. One problem is that we are caught up in the idea that we're "a team," which means we have to plan every expedition together and stick to it. We need to allow ourselves room to adapt. I feel that what I need to do right now is to stop all the activities I'm pursuing with my students around my current expedition—the human body—and let them explore one aspect of this extremely complex subject.

Another difficulty is that we are teaming almost exclusively on content. I should be able to get assistance with content from anyone in the building. I should be able to go to an upper-school science teacher and say, "I'm doing an expedition on the human body and I'd like you to do some animal dissection with us." Teaming should mean I can go to the expert in the school building who can help me with specific content. Unlike the upper-school teachers, who have more specialized interests, I have to teach all the subjects, so there's no way I can know everything I need to know. In the future, I hope our kindergarten–second-grade team can continue to team about content, but, more important, we should team about teaching, about expeditionary teaching, and observing each other's classrooms.

In summary, there are three things I take from these two expeditions and the differences between them. First, I learned the importance of a clear, well-designed project, one that serves both as a vehicle for exploring children's understandings of specific content, and as a final destination. Second, I want to continue to use the idea of public/private work to help my children grasp the importance of revision and standards. And third, I want to re-envision the way I use my peers so I broaden the points of connection between my work and theirs. I really need my team members to help me with my teaching, because they share the same issues; they know children at this age. But I don't want the learning to stop there. I want to reach outside my team to the experts in the building who can help me better understand how I can lead my students into rich, complex subject matter.

3

Making Theater, Making Sense, Making Change

Kathy Greeley

Middle school humanities teacher Kathy Greeley takes us through her own journey into a student-driven theater production, drawing on the roots of the Civil Rights movement and the Holocaust. Greeley initiates and guides students through the production, but they build the play together, drawing on students' work, class discussions, and readings from the curriculum. While talking about and reflecting on the qualities of a good production, students work collaboratively to write scenes, design and build the set, direct, and act in the play. Through the process of producing the play, the students gain insight into the relevance of history to their own lives.

It is opening night. The school cafeteria has been transformed. Strips of tarpaper seamed together with duct tape hide the institutional checkerboard floor. Suspended from the ceiling on window poles, large sheets of cotton muslin peopled with black silhouettes conceal the juice machine and cinderblock walls. I smile as I recognize Paul's high-top haircut and Marie's stocky figure permanently posed. Three trees of stage lights make the transformation complete. When the power is switched on, their rosy glare dictates the limits of another world.

The audience streams in noisily. Cast members are flitting about anxiously. We are trying to herd them "backstage" into the music room. I know I look calm, cheerful, confident. But inside, my stomach is churning. I go over in my head what I want to say to them. I have never had to do this alone before. In years past, there was Diana or Steve, experts, seasoned veterans, professionals who knew just the right thing to focus thirty-four young and very nervous performers. But this time I am on my own.

We begin with warm-ups, relying on routine to calm and center us. Next, a simple clapping game. I stand in the middle of the circle and begin to clap my hands over my head. As in Simon Says, they join in and catch the rhythm. The trick is to pay attention to when I do not clap. The first time I pause, there is a wide sprinkling of claps as those not focused continue in the rhythm. Giggles. The second time a handful of clapping bandits. A groan. The third pause is marked with a unified silence, and then a cheer.

"You are a remarkable group," I tell them. "Together, you have created more than a play, you have created a piece of art. Our play is about courage. You have all shown real courage by taking the risk to speak from your hearts. Because of that, your work will reach into the hearts of others. I have never seen a group of people work so well together. This was collaboration in the truest sense of the word. Be proud. And don't forget"—on this they all join in—"be loud, clear, and slow."

The cast files out silently to get into their positions. I take my seat, clutching the script. The lights dim to total blackness. The audience hushes. The music begins. And I watch magic unfold.

As I look back on that moment, I ask myself, "How did we ever do that? How did we build that trust, that willingness to take risks, that commitment to let go of our own personal investments and do what is best for the whole? How did we get thirty-four preadolescents to focus, to work together, to give voice to some of their deepest thoughts? It seems like magic."

I do believe in magic, but I do not believe magic just happens. Magic is made. Sorcerers know the steps. Certain potions must be mixed together, the ingredients have to be right. And, as the Sorcerer's Apprentice discovered, you cannot just open a book and follow the recipe. It takes time, support, experimentation, and guidance.

I am not a drama teacher. I teach seventh- and eighth-grade humanities, an integration of language arts and social studies, at the Graham and Parks School in Cambridge, Massachusetts. A kindergarten-to-eighth-grade alternative public school, Graham and Parks is located in a racially and economically diverse neighborhood, although students come from all parts of the city. There is also a large Haitian population, as the school houses the city's Haitian bilingual program. By the seventh and eighth grade, many bilingual students have joined mainstream, English-speaking classes. The seventh and eighth grade, unlike the lower grades, is partially departmentalized. I teach two different humanities sections, and because of the integration of language arts and social studies, I have a large block of time (one hundred minutes) with each group. This move toward integrated curriculum and longer teaching time was a critical prerequisite in being able to do activities and projects like the play.

I have always had a passion for history, a fascination with learning about and understanding people's lives in other times. Unfortunately, all my students did not share this view. They saw history as a string of events irrelevant to their own lives. I began to think that maybe if they could "try on" these other lives through theater, they would begin to see themselves as threads in a larger weave. Performance would not allow passivity or apathy. They would have to get engaged.

The problem was I knew nothing about theater. My biggest dramatic experience had been playing Blackbeard in our fifth-grade production of *Treasure Island*. I had three lines. I do not remember the lines, but I will never forget the exhilaration of performing them, or my pride in the cardboard waves we had laboriously painted. *Treasure Island* was one of the highlights of my entire school career.

Growing Through Uncertainty

I decided to take the plunge with *On the Line*, a play about the famous "Bread and Roses" strike of 1912. The play brought together themes we had been studying all semester: immigration, the Industrial Revolution, and the growth of the labor movement. Having no experience producing plays, I turned to the community to draw on the resources and expertise around us. A good friend, Diana Moller, who had taught theater for years (whose son coincidentally was in the class) agreed to help one day a week. Between us, we recruited a talented graduate student intern, a professional set designer from the Boston University theater, an artist who helped us construct our set, a local actor/director who shared his insights and expertise, a local musician who coached our "minstrels." Parents also joined the crew, helping with costumes, supervising set construction, and rehearsing lines with actors.

My goal was one of ownership. I did not just want my students to perform a play, I wanted them to shape it. The real work had to be done by the students themselves. We made many mistakes, and things did not always go smoothly. But in spite of the crises, or perhaps because of them, I watched a remarkable feeling grow among the members of the class. I saw them pull together, support each other, push each other, demand of each other and of themselves their very best. A transformation had taken place. Far from simply making history come alive, I discovered, this process of making theater made students come alive. And even though this was probably one of the most exhausting experiences of my teaching career, it made me come alive.

Over the years, since *On the Line*, a tradition of quality theater was established in my classroom. Two years ago, as my new students filed into the classroom in September, the questions started up before the students had even sat down. "Are we going to get to do a play this year?" "What play are we going to do?" "Can we write our own play this year?" "When are we going to do the play so I can tell my parents?" I knew they were hooked. I smiled at them confidently. But inside I was asking myself the same questions.

For the past three years, finding the right play to do had been fairly easy. But this year I was really stumped. Our curriculum theme for the year was change: How do societies change? How do people make change in their society? How are we changing? Luckily, I have a lot of freedom to develop and choose the curriculum. While some curriculum areas are recommended, there are no rigid requirements. I planned to begin the year with the Facing History and Ourselves curriculum. I had started teaching this curriculum six years earlier and had always been drawn to the way it helped adolescents reflect critically on key social issues and their own choices in life.

By using the rise of the Nazi Party in Germany in the 1930s and the resulting Holocaust as a historical case study of human behavior, the curriculum challenges students to reflect on the causes and consequences of present-day intolerance, violence, racism, and passivity. Students examine the social, political, and economic factors that led to the rise of the Nazi Party and the steps Hitler took to consolidate his power to create a dictatorship, including the role of propaganda, racial theories, and the roles of victims, victimizers, and bystanders during this period. Students are encouraged to identify parallels between this history and current events and to make connections to social responsibility, the importance of thinking for oneself, standing up for one's beliefs, and building a community committed to justice.

I then planned to shift to a study of the Civil Rights movement in the United States. We would try to place well-known events—our school was named after Rosa Parks and every child in it knows the story of the Montgomery, Alabama, bus boycott—within the complex framework that gave rise to those events. We would also look at how ordinary people, through remarkable acts of courage, were able to change history. The theme of change would link these different units.

As I spoke to friends and colleagues about ideas for a play, people would say, "Hey, there are lots of good plays for kids to do." But that was not the point. I was not interested in just putting on a play. There had to be a connection, an organic connection to the curriculum. The point of making theater was to reach inside ourselves, to reach out to our community, and to make sense of what we were learning. The material we were dealing with was both deeply disturbing and inspirational. And the issues of justice, power, and courage were richly compelling ones for my students.

It was clear to me that we had to do an original production again. But how? Where would the stories come from?

There is a wealth of stories in these histories. But unlike the year before with *Looking for America*, they were not our stories. I could not envision doing a play of Holocaust vignettes or trying to reenact the Civil Rights movement or antiwar protests on stage. I worried that the scale of those stories of life and death could too easily be trivialized. Our play had to be built from a place that the students could feel. When students would ask me, "What is our play going to be about?" I would just smile and say, "I don't know yet. We need to figure it out." During Open House in September, a parent asked expectantly, "Are you doing a play this year?"

"Of course," I answered.

"What is it going to be about?" another parent inquired.

"We don't know yet, but we'll keep you posted." I acted nonchalant, but inside I was panicked.

So we began the year not knowing—a very scary thing for a teacher, I think. But I was keeping my ears open, listening, waiting, trying to trust, and trying to keep my anxieties in check.

Rather than leaping into pre–World War II Germany, as I mentioned, Facing History begins with an exploration of some of the fundamental themes raised in the curriculum. We began the course by reading a newspaper article about the Kitty Genovese murder in Brooklyn, New York, in 1965. Thirty-eight people watched as a young woman was repeatedly stabbed. The police were called only after the victim was dead and her assailant had fled. Students, shocked by the story, struggled to understand. "Why didn't they do something?" "Why did people let this happen?" We began to brainstorm possible reasons for their lack of response. Was it fear, apathy, paralysis? "Maybe they thought someone else had already called the police." "Maybe they were afraid the killer would come after them." "Maybe they didn't know what to do." As we talked, the lines between right and wrong seemed very clear. Someone should have intervened.

"But, what if, during recess, you hear someone call someone else a nigger or a stupid Haitian? What would you do?" I asked. That is different, they replied. That is not murder.

"It's really none of my business," said Sarah Jane. "Kids do stuff like that all the time. You can't stop that."

"But how can you stop a murder if you can't even stop a 'dis'?" I persisted. "Being able to get involved, to do the right thing, to stand up for what you believe takes practice. If we can't act on the small things, how can we ever imagine we will act when the big ones happen?"

As we got deeper into our study of the Holocaust, these questions emerged over and over. Why did people let this happen? When must we act, and where do we find the courage to do so? Why did some people choose to perpetrate violence and hatred? How did others become targeted as the victim? And what about the majority of people who were simply bystanders?

In October we started experimenting with theater games once every week or two. The games pushed us to get out of our heads and into our bodies more, to stop thinking and just do. The process reminded me of freewriting or "writing to think." When you let go of your mind, amazing things will come out.

After each game, we would sit in a circle and talk about what we had learned from it and how it felt. One day we played a familiar observation game. Students got in pairs, and Diana asked them to turn around and change three things about themselves. Rings came off, shoes were untied, earrings disappeared. After a minute or two, they turned around and tried to guess what had changed about each person. "Okay," she said. "Now turn around again and change eight more things." Students groaned, but turned around. Sweatshirts came off, shoes were put on opposite feet, facial expressions changed. "Good," Diana said. "Now try changing fifteen more things." Before the protests could get very far, she interjected, "Just try it." Now things got really active. They took books from the bookshelf. They swapped clothing. They borrowed glasses and pencils from their neighbors. Postures changed. Different hands were leaned on.

"You see, you could do it!" Diana congratulated them. "That's lesson number one. Never say you can't do something. What else did you learn? How did you solve your problem? What did you draw on?"

"Well, first we changed things on ourselves," said Anna.

"Then what?" Diana coaxed.

"Then we stated using each other," ventured Emilio.

"Excellent; and finally? Where else did you turn?"

"To things—like books and pencils and stuff just lying around," Ariful responded.

"Exactly!" Diana exclaimed. "So that's the other lesson. When you run into a problem that you are trying to solve, there are three places to turn for answers: look inside yourselves, turn to each other, and use your environment."

We would also talk about what we needed from each other to make the process work. We needed to be willing to take risks, to try new things. We did not want to be laughed at for looking silly or making mistakes. We needed to focus and concentrate. We had to keep an open mind and not dismiss ideas with which we did not agree. We needed to trust each other and feel safe. We kept this list posted in the classroom as a reminder and added to it as necessary.

Emerging Consensus

In November we were fortunate to have a guest speaker from Facing History. Gregory Alan Williams is an African-American actor who lives in Los Angeles. During the Los Angeles riots of 1993, Williams saved the life of a Japanese-American man who was being brutally beaten by a mob at the infamous corner of Florence and Normandy streets. His book, *A Gathering of Heroes: Reflections on Rage and Responsibility,* described his experiences and the events in his own life that motivated him to act as a rescuer.

Williams has a commanding presence. With dramatic flair, he told about the rescue. But he also described having chosen not to help someone else in danger earlier that same day because "they were not my people." He told about being the victim of racial violence, but he also described being part of a group that severely beat a young man for the crime of being different. He spoke about standing against the mob, but he also remembered going along with the crowd. He challenged us to think about what a hero really is. Yes, someone who rushes into a burning building and saves a life is a hero. But what about a single mother who works day and night for years to support and sustain her children? Maybe that takes even more courage.

But how can we make a difference, the students asked. We are just kids. Williams replied, "If not you, then who? And if not now, when? You can't sit and wait for the 'right' moment. And you can't necessarily do it alone either. But if you are willing to speak out, to take a stand, then maybe another will be inspired to join you. And then another, and another. That's the 'power of we.' With the 'power of we,' you can make a difference."

When we got back to the classroom, the class was buzzing with energy. A deep chord had been struck. I grabbed a piece of newsprint and taped it up on the board. "What makes a hero?" I asked. "What is courage?" And the ideas flowed. Taking a stand for what you believe. Being willing to take a risk. Trying to live life by your principles. Giving other people hope. Admitting to having done wrong. Being honest with yourself. Taking responsibility for your actions and for others. Dedicating your life to something bigger than yourself. And the list went on. We had just a few minutes left when Emily raised her hand. "I think this is what our play should be about." The consensus was immediately apparent in all the nodding heads.

So we started to explore this idea of heroes. We made webs—a diagram that links different areas of knowledge around a theme—and students interviewed young children about who their heroes were and why. For several of those children, their heroes were in their own family: an older sister or brother, a parent. One six-year-old girl said, "My daddy is my hero because he is friendly and nice. And he listens to me." Another eight-year-old admired her dad because he "helps me with my homework, cooks good dinners, and kills spiders." For several children under seven, the Power Rangers were their heroes: they were "cool and strong," "saved people," "could do flips," and "had special powers."

Students interviewed their peers, and we mapped out all the data we collected. Different heroes emerged. For many, sports figures were big: Michael Jordan, Troy Aikman, Larry Bird, Julius Erving. They admired these athletes' determination, discipline, and talent. For others, political or Civil Rights activists stood out: Malcolm X, Martin Luther King, Gandhi. These people had sacrificed themselves to fight for the rights of oppressed peoples, people without power or privilege. And there were some more personal choices. One fourteen-year-old girl said she admired people with terminal illnesses who fought to live. A fourteen-year-old boy admired a friend who was in a band because "he is so good at what he does at such a young age."

In the Facing History curriculum we had also studied heroes such as Mordechai Anilewitz, a young man who led the Warsaw ghetto resistance, and Hannah Szenes, a young Palestinian Jewish poet who risked her life, parachuting behind Nazi lines to aid Jews. I asked students to think about what motivated each of these people to risk their lives by resisting Nazi control. Why did these particular individuals act when others did not? Ariful wrote about Anilewitz: "I think anger motivated Mordechai to fight back. At one point, he realized that they were all going to be killed, so he decided to go down fighting. Even though he knew he was going to die, he still wanted to live. He didn't want to just save himself because he cared about his fellow Jews."

"I think that Hannah Szenes was a hero because she risked her life to save others," wrote Jash. "She was very courageous when she didn't give the radio code even when they tortured her and when they threatened to kill her mother. When the hangman killed her, she refused to put on the blindfold. She did all of this because she wanted other people to have the chance to taste freedom. This is why I think that she was a hero."

Students shared their profiles through brief dramatic presentations. Working in small groups, they had to think about the essence of each hero's action and portray that moment. It could be the moment that Anilewitz decided to take his own life rather than turn himself in to the Gestapo. But students had to choose that essential moment, imagine the characters that would be involved, and set the scene in a physical space and time.

As we discussed courage, we also talked about fear. Did heroes feel no fear? Or was real courage overcoming our fears? We wrote "Five-Sense" poems about fear. The poem emerges from a series of questions: What color is it? What does it smell like? What does it sound like? What does it taste like? What does it feel like to the touch? How does it make you feel? Carrie wrote:

Fear is dark blue and brown
musty and sweaty, sticky and rotten,
a drum beating, pounding
a salty taste.
I can't swallow it
because it is a knot
tied deep inside of me.

We also made body sculptures. Students worked in pairs in which one student was the "clay" and the other the "sculptor." The "sculptor" shaped the "clay" into his or her interpretation of fear. Bodies twisted, hands were raised, heads turned away. The pairs switched, and we then tried sculpting courage. Arms reached out, backs straightened, heads were raised. And we talked. What is it young adolescents most fear? "Getting shot," said Troy, an eighth-grade African-American boy. Troy is usually one of the jokesters of the class. But this time he was not laughing. "What other people think of you," said Leana, a tall, willowy girl, a dancer. Others nodded. We added to the list: looking different, being left out, secrets becoming public, wearing the right clothes, getting picked on by bigger kids, gangs, war. There were a lot of things to fear.

The year was moving along. We finished Facing History in January and began working on the roots of the Civil Rights movement. Using the model of our Holocaust study, we started looking for key elements of when and where the seeds were planted. What were the social, political, and economic conditions that gave rise to a movement for justice, equality, and change? We went back to the Civil War, the Reconstruction Era, the beginning of Jim Crow, and key rulings of the Supreme Court. Each student picked a topic that interested him or her, such as the origins and growth of the Ku Klux Klan, African Americans in the military, the Harlem Renaissance, the founding and development of the NAACP. They researched, wrote about, and presented their topics, as experts, to the class. Students were beginning to see that, once again, history was complex, events and people influenced each other, and significant periods of change did not just happen.

It was now February, and we still did not have a script. We did not even have a story yet. But we had been gathering material, collecting pieces of ideas and experiences, generating building blocks of writing, research, techniques, and process. The students kept asking when we would start working on the play.

"We are working on the play," I would answer.

"Yeah, but when are we *really* going to work on the play? You know, write the script, cast the parts, rehearse, make the set?"

"Soon; trust me," I would say, trying to keep my own anxieties under control and my mind open.

That month we were lucky to have another visit from Gregory Alan Williams. This time he came as a playwright consultant. "So, what's your play about?" he asked.

"It's about heroes and courage and change and . . . well, we don't know everything yet. We don't have a script yet." Embarrassed giggles. A few of them glare accusingly at me.

"That's okay. What is it you want to say to your audience? What is your message?" he pushed.

"Well, uh . . . we kind of want to talk about perpetrators, victims, and bystanders and . . ." Embarrassed giggles.

"That's a good place to start. Have any of you ever been a victim, a perpetrator, or a bystander?" Embarrassed silence. He persisted. "Has anyone ever made fun of you or put you down? How about you?" He looked at Brady, a gangly seventh grader whose long hair usually hangs down to his chin, hiding his eyes. Brady rose to the occasion.

"Yeah, I guess. Sometimes other kids make fun of me because I like to wear my hair long. Usually it doesn't bother me, but every once in a while it does."

Williams nodded sympathetically and said softly, "Brady, can you *show* us how it feels, those times when it really gets to you? Show us with your body?" Brady stood up awkwardly. I was watching intently. So was the rest of the class. This was a boy who barely speaks in class. He struck a pose. His head down and knees slightly bent, his hands held an invisible burden over his back, like a wretched Santa Claus. There was silence, and Brady continued to hold his position. "Thank you, Brady," Williams said quietly. "That was terrific." The class burst into applause.

Williams asked for another volunteer to share an experience as a perpetrator. Troy stood up, pointed his finger at an invisible target, half covered a smirking smile with his hand, cocked his head. Williams silently motioned Brady into Troy's line of vision. A picture was coming into focus. "How about a bystander?" Anna, a very bright but somewhat withdrawn seventh grader, stood up, circling the two boys for a minute and then stopped, just outside their sphere. She turned her body away, put her hands up to shield her eyes, but was surreptitiously watching. The triangle was complete.

Looking at the tableau, we recognized that each of us had been, at least once in our lives, in each point of that triangle. We all knew the powerlessness of the victim. We knew the inflated self-importance of the perpetrator. But most deeply resonant was the distance of the bystander. How many times had we heard a remark that made us uncomfortable but said nothing? How many times had we witnessed an incident we wanted to interrupt or intervene in, but did not know how? How many times had we gone along with the crowd, afraid of being singled out? As one German citizen reflecting back on the Nazi era said, "Suddenly it all comes down, all at once. You see what you are, what you have done, or more accurately, what you haven't done. For that was all that was required of most of us: that we do nothing."

As the class looked at the tableau, we realized that we had found our focus. Like a string in sugar water, this tableau became the anchor around which ideas crystallized. Our play would be about this relationship: the victim, the perpetrator, and, primarily, the bystander.

Constructing the Play

The time had come to begin constructing the play. Diana came back to help us shape, mold, and fashion all the pieces into a cohesive whole. To remind ourselves what we had to work with, we wrote on newsprint a list of all the activities and exercises we had conducted: fear poems, body sculptures, resister and rescuer skits and profiles, hero webs and interviews, superhero and other improvs, folk tales of courage, mirroring exercises, "sound" theater, and student writing about changing, witnessing prejudice, and being afraid.

Then Diana asked, "What is someone called who writes plays?"

"A playwright," a number of students called out.

"Spell it for me," she said.

"P-L-A-Y-W-R-I-G-H-T."

"Great," she said. "Can anyone tell me why it isn't spelled P-L-A-Y-W-R-I-T-E?" I was stumped. Not only did I not know why, I had never even wondered why. "Can you think of any other jobs people do who are called 'something-wright'?"

"A shipwright?"

"Yes! And what does a shipwright do?"

"They build ships."

"Yes, and playwrights build plays. As you begin to work on actually writing your play, think of it as building something together. You will mold and shape it. A basic form will emerge, you will make many changes before it is finished. Now, what kind of play do you want to build?"

We started brainstorming all our hopes for this production. It should be mainly about young people, but there could also be adult characters. It should take place partly in the present, but should incorporate the lessons of the histories we had been learning. It had to be funny, but it also had to deal with serious issues. It should not paint things as good versus bad. Life is more complex than that. They did not want to offer pat answers, they wanted to ask questions ("We don't want it to be like an afterschool special."). They wanted the audience to leave thinking.

After this meeting, Diana and I started drafting a storyline. This was a major leap. After months of soliciting ideas, inviting feedback, turning ownership over to the students, I worried that there would be a reaction to our taking such a unilateral step. Would there be a power struggle? Would they feel the adults had taken over the process?

Our first draft was rejected. But it was not rejected for any of the reasons I had worried about. On the contrary, the students welcomed the structure. As adults know, it is usually much easier to work from something concrete and make changes than to expect something to emerge from a large group. The story just was not saying what they felt they wanted to say.

Back to the drawing board. I kept trying to pull from that visual image of our tableau. Someone becomes a bystander when he or she witnesses an incident, an act, and fails to get involved. It seemed that our play had to start with some kind of incident. I thought back to an incident that had actually occurred during the beginning weeks of school in September. A group of students, several of whom were in my classes, had started chasing another seventh-grade boy—in fun, they said. But it had turned ugly. Once the group cornered him, a crowd had gathered that egged them on to beat him up. These were not "bad" students. They had intended no harm. But something had happened to them that they could not explain or even understand at the time.

I started running ideas by as many people as would listen to me. One Sunday morning, as I was sitting in a café with a friend, jotting notes on a small paper napkin, the pieces began to fall together. I rushed home to bang out Draft Number Two and presented it the next day to my classes.

"Okay, listen to this." I started reading my notes. "There is an explosion of activity on stage. A group of kids are chasing another kid. They catch him and beat him up. The audience gets the idea of a violent act with a victim and a group of perpetrators, but no faces are seen. In the next scene, lights come up on a school cafeteria. The students are buzzing with excitement. We focus in on three kids who are talking ("Did you hear what happened yesterday?"). As they talk, they reveal what they know about "the incident" from a certain perspective. At least one of them was witness to the incident. They think the victim got what he deserved. We shift to another location (recess, hallway), and we hear the story again from other students, who this time are more sympathetic to the victim. A few of these students were also witnesses. Do we have a third scene? We then shift to the teachers' room to hear a few teachers talking about the same incident—this time in simplistic terms ("Those kids are such bullies.").

"Of all the kids who were witnesses [bystanders], there are two or three who begin to wonder if they have done the right thing by saying and doing nothing. Each one turns to her or his hero to ask advice about what to do. Each kid's hero takes her or him on a journey to a place where, in spite of the risks, a person has decided to 'do the right thing.' One scene visits the Holocaust and a resister, one scene visits the Civil Rights movement, and maybe one takes a present-day person's story. In the next scenes, we need to see these students back in their own environment, but somehow they have to change or act differently, though in small ways. Somehow the kids should come together, but I don't know how."

As I was reading the outline to the class, I glanced up to see heads nodding in approval. "That's much better than the last one." "Yeah, that's good." But then came the questions: "What is the incident going to be?" "What are the kids who go to 'heroland' like?" "Who are the heroes?" "What stories do the bystanders visit?" "How is it going to end?" I responded, "I don't know the answers to those questions. We are going to have to figure them out together." But we now had a rough draft. A real place to start. A skeleton to flesh out. And we had consensus. We were headed in the right direction.

It seemed that we should be building from the guts of the play rather than starting at the beginning. And the guts of the play were the "heroland" stories about courage that were rooted in our historical study. We had to make sure that the lessons each bystander learned from his or her journey would have meaning for that character and for the incident. Because we were dealing with real stories, we had to choose carefully the story that demonstrated an important message.

We decided to look first at the Holocaust stories of resisters and rescuers. We got out all the profiles students had written in the fall, spread them out on a table, and started reading them over again. Once students had had a chance to refresh their memories, they broke into groups of four and had to pick the story they felt had the best message for the play. They had to identify the elements of courage embodied in the story and then develop a skit that illustrated these elements. I reminded them that they needed to be thinking about what best served the play and not necessarily the story they found most interesting or thrilling. For example, some students really liked the story of Joseph Gani, a young Hungarian Jew who joined a desperate rebellion in one of the concentration camps. The class admired his refusal to be a victim and his decision to fight back even when there was no hope of winning. But the group decided the hopelessness of his situation was not what we wanted to communicate to our audience.

Two stories emerged as our final candidates. The first was the story of Oskar Schindler. We had read about Schindler, and some students had seen Stephen Spielberg's movie *Schindler's List*. They were intrigued with the way Schindler had changed from being purely out for himself to risking his privilege, his fortune, and ultimately his life to be a rescuer. They also admired how he stood up for others and used his position of power to help. His story fit our themes of change and courage well. The second candidate was the story of Andre and Magda Trocme. In full view of the Vichy government and Nazi SS, the Trocmes led the people of their village, Le Chambon, in southern France, to save thousands of Jewish children and adults from certain death. The Trocmes, and most of the village, were Huguenots and had known persecution in Catholic France. They drew strength from their own oppression to fight against the oppression of others. The story of Le Chambon also embodied the "power of we" that Gregory Alan Williams had spoken about. There was not one hero who saved the day, but rather a whole group of people who, inspired by the courage and commitment of the Trocmes, agreed to work together to do what they could to oppose violence and destruction.

We discussed at length which story would work best in our play. In the end, the students chose the Trocmes and the village of Le Chambon. They liked the message that by coming together people can make a difference in the lives of others, even when the odds are so overwhelming. We also found the Trocme improvs worked better. Students had had a hard time capturing the importance of Schindler's story in just one scene. It had taken Spielberg a whole movie to do it; how could we do it better? Finally, we decided it was important to have a story that was less known to people. We wanted people to know there were many unsung heroes.

Now that we had a story, we began to build the scene. We went back to the original improvs the small groups had done. Two groups had worked on the Trocme story. One scene took place in the Trocme kitchen, with

Andre and Magda talking about the problems and dangers they had encountered that day. The second scene showed Andre taking two Jewish children door to door through the village until he found a family who could take them in. Which one did we like better? Both scenes conveyed important information about the story to the audience. The kitchen scene gave the characters an opportunity to share the inner thoughts of these two people. The night visit scene dramatized the involvement of the whole village. Why not blend them together, we decided.

Previously, when any improvs or scenes were shared, my mantra had been, "What works?" We rarely discussed what had not worked. That was usually fairly obvious. By focusing primarily on the strengths of an improv, we achieved two important goals. First, students overcame their fears of performing, of being judged or laughed at. A sense of trust and confidence grew in the classroom, encouraging everyone to take risks. Second, we gradually built an awareness of what makes good theater. "I liked how you really stayed in character the whole time." "Your facial expressions were great. We really knew what you were thinking without your saying a word." "I loved how you had the characters flash back to an earlier time right in the middle of the scene."

As we began to mold the scenes for the play, I was struck by how good my students were at giving each other supportive, insightful feedback. I realized that they were simply transferring a skill we had been working on all year to making theater. In the beginning of school, we had analyzed a wide range of student-written stories to identify the elements of good writing. We had introduced response groups for the writing process. We had strict rules about being respectful, considerate, focusing on the positive first, and giving concrete, constructive feedback. Students had used this format to critique projects as well as writing. Whenever we did projects, we would discuss criteria for excellence. How do we know we have done quality work? What are the elements to be striving for?

Something different was happening. I had always been committed to writing as a process and to response as a critical part of that process. But it did not always come easily with students. Many were afraid at first to share their work. Some students were comfortable with giving others feedback, but some rarely contributed. Others had to be continually reminded of the rules. There were days when one or another response group worked really well, but I was always wondering just how deeply the process had sunk in. But as we worked together on scenes for the play, a new feeling emerged. It was like taking the training wheels off a bike and riding freely. The supports, the reminders, the attention to the structure just melted away as we all became engrossed in the product. Finally, the process was working, really working.

I have wondered why this transformation happened. Was it because the groundwork had been laid in the fall and it finally kicked in? Or was it easier to critique unwritten work? Did it have to do with a group presenting work as opposed to an individual? Was it a matter of ownership? Or was it the nature of the work itself? This play was our creation. It expressed our inner thoughts and emotions. Other people were going to see it. The stakes were high. I imagine that all these factors entered in. My gut sense was that the authenticity, the trueness, the deep meaning of the work was the real catalyst. We were committed to high-quality work. The class understood that getting feedback, shaping, and reworking was the way to reach the standard we had set for ourselves.

Having decided to blend the two scenes, we referred the scene to a committee of writers. A small group of students (including two who had originally researched the Trocmes) went off to develop the scene further and to write a first draft of the script. Through discussion, they decided that the danger the Trocmes had lived with on a daily basis had to be demonstrated in the scene. Two new characters were thus added: Gestapo agents who barge into their home. They engaged the characters in various improvisational dialogues. What would Magda say when Andre returns an hour late one evening? How would she be feeling? What would the children feel when they first met these two strangers? What is the relationship between them? How do they react when Nazis appear suddenly at the door?

While the Trocme scene was growing, the rest of the class turned its attention to the preceding scene. In this scene, we would meet one of the bystanders who had witnessed the incident and was disturbed by his own failure to act. Who would this person be? Why would he be questioning his own behavior? What is his relationship to the victim? To the perpetrators? What hero visits him? How will he change? Since the Huguenots of Le Chambon had been motivated to act as rescuers because of their own persecution, we decided this character would similarly be motivated by his or her own experience of being a victim. As we looked back over our charts of superheroes, we decided to have the character meet the Pink Power Ranger, a popular superhero of the younger set. Two volunteers jumped up to try improvising.

"Where will this scene take place?" I asked. "What makes sense?"

"Adam should be coming home from school."

"Okay, let's help him out a bit. How is Adam feeling when he gets home?"

"Frustrated."

"Angry."

"Upset."

"Okay. Think frustrated, angry, upset, Adam. Now, what can he be doing? What is the first thing you do when you get home?"

"Get something to eat."

"Okay. Let's see what happens." Adam walked onto the "set." "How did you get in?" I asked. "Can we see you coming through the door?" He started again. "Pretend you can't find your key," someone called out. He looked for his key to open the door. He could not find the key. He rummaged through his pockets, his bookbag, his pockets again. His frustration was mounting. He pounded on the "door." The class was cracking up. He called, "MOM? MOM?! ANYBODY HOME?" Pounded again. Someone called out, "Look under the mat!" He looked under the "doormat," found the key finally, and stumbled into the house. He dropped his bag in the "kitchen" and mimed going into the refrigerator. "Okay, who drank all the d—— Pepsi?" he muttered. He got out a milk carton, poured a glass, took a long drink—and gagged. "This milk is disgusting!" he cried. Then he went to make a sandwich. The jelly jar was stuck closed. The peanut butter jar was empty. He exploded in frustration. The class exploded in hysterics. Another scene was coming to life.

Recently, as I was trying to write about the making of this scene, I went back to Adam. "Was this how it happened, how this scene came together?" I asked. "Yeah, sort of," Adam responded. "I remember someone telling me to check under the doormat. But I don't think that I did all those things right away. I kept doing it over and over again. Each time we added something else in. People kept giving suggestions, and it kept building. I didn't think all those things up on my own."

Another group started working on the second "heroland" visit. This scene would take place during the Civil Rights movement. We chose the story of Mose Wright, the uncle of a fourteen-year-old African-American boy named Emmett Till who was brutally murdered one night by a group of white men in Mississippi in 1955. Young Till made the mistake of saying, "Bye, baby," to a white woman in a store. Mose Wright, under the threat of losing his life, stood up in court to point out the murderers. Students were inspired by this story. Through our studies of the roots of the Civil Rights movement and reading *To Kill a Mockingbird*; *Roll of Thunder, Hear My Cry*; and *I Know Why the Caged Bird Sings*, they understood the depth of this old man's courage.

This time, the whole class worked on ideas for the scene. Students divided into three groups, and each one developed a scene that focused on the essential message of the story. We then presented each one and discussed what worked well. While all the scenes had similar elements, each one introduced an interesting twist. One scene started with the accused white men meeting with their lawyer, who confidently assured them that they had nothing to worry about. Another scene used a court clerk to establish time and place. A third interjected a flashback of Till being forced out of Wright's house in the middle of the night. All these ideas were eventually incorporated into the final scene.

As students experimented with improvisations, I took copious notes on each character created, every good line, every suggestion that worked, as many stage directions as I could remember. For some scenes, students went off in pairs or small groups (as in the Trocme scene) and developed a draft of the script. I would draft other scenes from the improv and bring the script back the next day for critique. I worried, again, that students might resent the loss of control over the process. But the students nearly always felt that I had been able to capture their words, their characterizations, their intentions on paper. And that was fine. The distinction between student and teacher was beginning to disappear. It was not their play or my play. We were a real team, with the goal of making the best product we could.

By the end of two weeks, we had a script: a story with seven scenes and twenty-seven characters. The play opens on an empty stage. As the lights come up, a slow-walking boy named Robert is being hailed: "Yo, Robert! We just want to talk to you!" Robert runs but cannot escape. Five students close in on him. In slow motion, they begin beating him down. Other characters quietly file in behind, watching. The attackers fade away, leaving the victim crumpled in the center of the stage. The bystanders, one by one, turn their backs.

The next day the school is abuzz with rumors. We begin to hear, from various points of view, about "the incident." Some feel the victim got what he deserved for "talking trash" about another student, claiming she was being beaten by her father. Others are more sympathetic. A few are neutral. Two characters, Janessa and Marcus, leave the scene feeling bothered. They turn to superheroes for answers. Marcus, at home alone in his kitchen, begins talking to his younger sister's Pink Power Ranger doll. Janessa, shooting hoops with her nerf ball in her bedroom, tells herself that Michael Jordan would know what to do. Both heroes magically appear and try to offer solace. But the Pink Power Ranger cannot give any advice. Television heroes are not like real heroes, she explains. The scriptwriters tell her what to do, good always wins out over evil, and everyone lives happily ever after. Michael Jordan sees solutions through his endorsement products. "Maybe you should get some Nikes and run away fast."

Failing to provide answers, each superhero takes his or her new friend on a journey through time. Marcus and the Pink Power Ranger visit the

Trocme house and witness how they provide shelter to Jews escaping the Nazis. Janessa and Michael Jordan go to Money, Mississippi, in 1955 to see the trial where Mose Wright testified. In the conclusion of the story, Janessa and Marcus, back at school, are challenged to put their lessons of courage and real heroism into practice. As Robert enters the cafeteria alone, Marcus's friends begin to mock him and call him a "faggot." Marcus objects to their language and tells them to leave the poor kid alone. Janessa, watching Marcus with his friends, simply gets up from her table and goes and sits defiantly with Robert. While neither is ready to take on the world, they both are willing to take small steps.

Casting: Lessons in Decision Making

There were some rough spots, and we were still missing our final scene, but we now had a real script to work from. We knew how many characters we had, and who they were, and we knew where and when the scenes took place. We knew enough to move to the next step—production.

We formed five different committees: assistant directors, set design and construction, costumes, music, and publicity. As in every other year, everyone would act. You could request a large part or a smaller part, but everyone had to walk on stage and say at least one line. Students were invited to sign up for the committee that interested them. The next day, we met in our committee groups. The set design crew went to investigate our performance space (the school cafeteria); the costume committee went to the library to check out books on World War II to see how people dressed then; the publicity crew started brainstorming ideas and designs for the poster; and the assistant directors gathered to make up a list of the characters they needed to cast.

Casting has always been done democratically in our plays. Each student is given a list of characters and is asked to rank the ones he or she is interested in playing. We then make a grid with every character on one axis and every member of the class on the other and we fill in the chart according to each student's request. The assistant directors work as a group to cast the parts. I instruct them to use two guidelines in their casting decisions. First, they should think about who can play which part best. We do not audition for roles. Because we have been doing improvs and role-plays for months and because the students have created and experimented with the characters, the assistant directors have a good sense of each student's talents. Second, they should try to honor people's requests for particular parts. But ultimately they need to make decisions in the best interest of the play as a whole.

I maintain the right of final veto or ultimate decision making, but I have never used it. In our first play, *On the Line*, the students cast a Haitian girl who had just been mainstreamed into an English-speaking classroom in a major role. Although they had rarely heard her speak, they thought her personality really fit the character. They also cast a boy with a serious speech disability as a union organizer who had a one-and-a half-page monologue. In each case, they recognized the risks, but felt that with support and practice Jodelle and Chris would be great in the parts. They were right. Jodelle never dropped a line, and Chris delivered his speech from a soapbox without faltering. Later, when asked how he felt about doing the play, Chris wrote, "I felt like a knight in shining armor and I could do anything!" I was convinced that our process worked.

This year, we ran into a different problem with casting. There were two boys and two girls who had chosen to be assistant directors. The two girls had both requested one of the lead acting roles. Usually I would not encourage directors also to take on leading parts, but this time they were the only two girls in the class who wanted the role. Similarly, the two boys had also requested a particular part, along with two other students in the class. I wondered how this situation would resolve itself. Would they use their power to cast themselves in the roles they wanted? Or would they try to think about what was best for the class, and the play, as a whole?

They made their grid, and I suggested they start with the easy decisions and work their way up to the hard ones. Finally, they had cast all the roles but the ones they had asked for. They talked about who was best for what part. They talked about what role they could give people who did not get the parts they wanted. They were very concerned that people feel satisfied with their final assignment. They did not want to waste any talent, and they did not want to hurt anyone's feelings. They were stuck.

"Tell us what to do," they said.

"I can't," I replied. "Directors get faced with tough decisions sometimes. You can't just back off when the going gets tough. Anyway, I don't know what the right decision is either. You have to find a way to make a decision. We can't go on with the play until this is resolved."

We decided to take the dilemma to the rest of the class. Who did they think should play the part? Should we take a vote? Should we audition this time? How can we decide? The class responded, "You are the directors. You should decide, not us. We trust that you'll make the best decision for the play." The student directors caucused again and still could not decide. Finally, I suggested they divide up. The girls should choose the part for the boys, and the boys should choose the part for the girls. They agreed. After about ten minutes of agonizing, each group finally made a decision. There was great excitement for those who got the parts they wanted; there was tremendous disappointment for those who did not. But having been part of the process, the students were able to put their personal desires aside in favor of what was best for the whole. The decision had been made, and we moved on.

I was continually struck throughout this play at how committed students were to the big picture. Often young people (and adults) can get very invested in their particular contribution, and have a harder time seeing what's best for the whole. I had struggled with this myself. I had had certain ideas about staging or set design which the students either resisted or sometimes flat out rejected. When I tried to force it, I saw it as just that—a force fit. The students instincts were right; I too needed to stay open to our collective wisdom.

Another major example of this commitment to the whole was when we were developing the ending scenes of the play. We wanted to show how Marcus's journey to the Trocme household had changed him. We wanted to give him an opportunity to move beyond his role as a bystander and take a stand for what he knew was right. One group had come up with a good idea. On his way home from school, Marcus runs into a few of his buddies outside a video store. They invite him to go in the store with him. He realizes that they are planning to steal a tape. He refuses to join them and tells them they are wrong to do it. They call him a goody-goody and go in anyway.

The class really liked the scene. It was realistic, and it did not have a happy ending in that Marcus was not able to convince the others to do the right thing. But still, he had made a stand at the risk of being seen as a wimp. It was a good scene. But as we put it together with the rest of the scenes, we realized it was unnecessary. It was taking the message that had been suggested in the scene before and making it totally explicit for the audience. Did we want to hit the audience over the head with our message? Or did we want to leave them pondering? We went back to our original goals to remind ourselves that we had wanted the audience to leave thinking. We did not want to wrap up our story neatly like an afternoon television special. After much discussion and debate, the class agreed to drop the scene. It was not easy to do, but we knew the play would be better without it.

One day, as we began to prepare for actual rehearsals, the assistant directors came to me. They were worried. None of them had ever directed before, and they were anxious that their peers would not listen to them. Their fears were legitimate. In other plays, we had at times had problems with actors who refused to take direction from their student directors. We had also had the reverse problem of student directors who became a bit intoxicated with their power over their peers. At least a couple of our directors this year had dictatorial tendencies and throughout the year had not been particularly supportive or constructive in their feedback to others. I agreed it would be wise to deal with the actor/director relationship before it became a crisis.

We called a class meeting, and the directors shared their concerns with the class. We then put up two pieces of newsprint saying, "What do directors need from actors?" and "What do actors need from directors?" We began to discuss the relationship and identified key elements that would make it work. Directors needed actors to focus, to cooperate, to be prepared, to be willing to try something risky, to keep an open mind, to trust the director's judgment. Actors needed from directors patience, suggestions rather than orders, constructive criticism, willingness to listen, support for building self-confidence, agreement not to abuse their position of authority. The bottom line for both groups was to feel respected.

This twenty-minute discussion changed the tenor of rehearsals. Although we had our difficult moments and our frustrations, there was an underlying sense of trust that we were all in this together. I watched students really push each other—to articulate lines more clearly, to slow down, to use silence, to let go of self-consciousness, to take tremendous risks. When tensions arose or relationships were strained, we would go back to our lists (which we kept posted in the classroom). We were all trying to make the play work. With the commitment to process, we were able to keep our eyes on the prize.

Opening night was a week away, and scene 8, the final scene of the play, had still not been written. In this scene, students wanted to speak directly to the audience about their own experiences, their own learning. They wanted to leave the audience thinking, thinking hard about their own choices and actions in life. But we had not figured out just how to do this. Several ideas had been floated, but nothing felt quite right.

"What do we do about scene 8?" I asked the class.

"We should ask the audience questions," said Emily, an outspoken eighth grader.

"What kinds of questions?" I responded.

"Well, like what would they do in those situations. Or maybe we should talk about the real-life things that happen to us all the time. Or maybe . . . oh, I don't know."

"Okay," I said. "Just try this. For homework tonight, write down how you think we should end the play. Or write down questions you would like to ask the audience. Or write down an incident that happened to you or a friend. Just write down some thoughts about the ending and we'll see what we get."

The next day a jumble of responses came in. Some students had written down simple questions like "What would you do if you were Janessa or Marcus?" Others had staging ideas: "Each person should stand in front of someone in the audience and look right at them." Some had written about their own experiences as bystanders and how they hoped they would now act differently. How could we put this all together in a way that made any sense?

As I leafed through the papers, I started to jot down questions or phrases that stood out to me. I started remembering lines from poems we had read, stories told by witnesses, reflections of survivors, excuses people had offered for inaction, excerpts from the students' writing from earlier in the year. Beginning with the famous quote from the Reverend Martin Niemöller, "First they came for the Communists, but I wasn't a Communist so I said nothing," I started weaving these strands together, interspersing lines like "Mind your own business," "We wear the mask," and "I don't want to get involved," with the students' own experiences:

> One time I was out trick-or-treating. We were about a block from my house. When this group of bigger kids started saying things like, "Oh, I remember him. He's that fat faggot." They came by me and grabbed my bag. I resisted, but they took it anyway. Nobody helped me.

I also reached back into the Facing History curriculum to draw on the lessons of the past. As a university professor tried to explain his failure to take a stand against the Nazi regime:

> Each act, each occasion was worse than the last. But only a little worse. You wait for the next, and the next. You wait for one great shocking occasion, thinking that others, when such a shock comes, will join with you in resisting.

And I took lines from their own wishes, dreams, hopes and fears: "Will anyone remember the poems I wrote? Or will they be burned in a bonfire in the back of their minds?" and "What's that you say? Another child blown away in the crossfire of gang warfare?" and "I don't want to be another statistic or a number without a name." A scene began to take shape.

The next day, I brought in my draft. I was nervous about how the kids would respond. Was I conveying their message? Or mine? They listened intently as I read it aloud. With the final lines, "Then they came for me, and there was no one left to speak for me," the class broke into applause. That night,

Nierika wrote in her journal, "Today we worked on scene 8. I love [underlined four times] that scene. It'll bring the audience to tears! It is a great way of 'wrapping it all up.' It ties all the themes of the play together so that it'll move the audience and they'll be thinking about it for a while!"

As rehearsals progressed and the set came together and costumes and props piled up in the room, I felt a strange sense of calm. Usually, the week before the show, panic sets in. You are always wishing you had just one more week to prepare. You cannot imagine that the set is going to be finished. You do not know where the music for the last scene is going to come from. You realize how one scene really has not received the attention it needs. It would be false to say that I was not anxious. But there was a calm that came from another place. Whether or not the play worked (and I was praying that it would), I knew the *process* had worked. I had witnessed deep thinking and honest struggle around tough issues of standing up for what you believe, for acting on your convictions, for not going along with the crowd. Not only did the students understand the history, they were responding to it every day in how they worked together. We had built a strong community in our classroom. I saw students supporting each other, encouraging each other to take risks, giving each other positive feedback, honest critique, and encouragement. I saw that they saw they could trust each other and count on each other. I saw that the class members had not just learned about history, but had come to own it for themselves. I was calm because I knew we had already been victorious.

The play was a huge success. As the lights dimmed on the final lines of scene 8, there was a hush in the cafeteria and then the audience burst into applause. I looked around to see people wiping tears from their eyes, just as Nierika had predicted. I saw cast members hugging each other, parents hugging kids, kids from the audience hugging the actors. We had just witnessed a powerful piece of magic.

Reflecting on Meaning and Change

The days after the play glowed. The students basked in their success. They felt good about themselves and good about each other. They recognized what they had achieved. But I wondered, What had they learned? What lessons would stay with them beyond the excitement of the play? How deep did the learning go?

Two months later, in June, I asked students to reflect on their experiences over the year and to think about what important lessons they had learned. I was deeply moved by their responses. Nierika wrote: "The most valuable experience that I have had all year was definitely the play. I had never done anything like it before, so everything was new to me. I enjoyed directing a lot and I think I did a good job at it. I also liked acting and writing parts of the play. But my favorite part of the whole experience was the feeling I got after one of our performances. I felt proud. I felt more pride than I'd felt for almost anything in my whole life. I was proud of myself, I was proud of you, but most of all I was proud of the class as a whole. It was amazing to realize what a great thing we could create by working together."

Carrie, who played Janessa, wrote: "When I think about risks I think about important things that happened to me. I think about the play, I think about class discussions we had, I think about the opinions that I defended, but most of all I think about what I learned about taking risks, and how hard it is to fight for what you believe in, but how important it is to take those risks."

Emilio wrote: "I know that I can now try to help other people and try to solve problems in my life a little better. I am learning not to be a bystander, but I haven't been able to show this. I have never done anything to stop a fight before . . . but I have grown to the point where I want to do something."

But perhaps the most eloquent response came from Emily, a quiet seventh grader who had struggled all year with being sure of herself:

I only hope that everyone learned as much as I did from The Incident *and that they took it back in their heads or hearts, because although you don't always think with your head, your heart is always in what you say.*

I say all this because today at lunch I was sitting with a kid who was in the play and he said, "He's gay," and I do not mean in the sense that yes, he was homosexual or yes, he is happy, but I mean in the insult form. I jumped on him (verbally). "Do you remember anything from the play?" I sat back as two others (one who had been in the play and one who had seen it) also made angry remarks about his bad choice of words. I don't remember his exact response, but it was something like "Yeah, you're right. Sorry." This is true! The names are withheld to protect the guilty, who apologized. I was freaked out that someone (especially someone who was in the play) would say that, but I was glad, ecstatic almost, that at least three people objected to his actions and he did apologize and realize what he had done.

I realize while typing these words that I myself am a perpetrator, we all are. At least once in some point in everyone's life you will hurt someone . . . But now that I know that, I can work to not hurt anyone in the future. I hate being labeled. I shall not label others. I hate being teased. I shall not tease others. I hate it when people joke about my shortness, which I cannot change. I shall not joke about others' physical features they cannot change. I hate being judged unfairly. I shall not unfairly judge others. And I shall never ever steal from others their pride, dignity, or happiness.

As I look back over this year, I realize that there were two important forces at work in creating this powerful learning experience for both my students and myself. The first was a rich and deep curriculum that tapped into critical issues in young people's lives: justice, courage, freedom, and personal responsibility. Facing History helped students to confront the complexities of history in ways that promoted critical and creative thinking.

But the content alone was not what moved Emily to a place where she could act to interrupt intolerance. Through the process of creating a play, students were able to make their own meaning from the lessons of history. They were able to put this meaning into practice. Not only did students learn about people who had taken risks in the past, they learned how to take risks themselves. They read about people who had asked questions and looked critically at personal choices, and they looked deeply into themselves. As they learned about people who had worked together for a better world, they worked together to experience the "power of we" for themselves. The curriculum gave them the examples from the past and inspired a hope for the future. The play provided a forum in which they could demonstrate to themselves, and to others, the power they have to make change.

4

Something from Nothing: An Expedition Into Economy, Community, and History

Steven Levy

In the following pages, fourth-grade teacher Steven Levy tells the story of a learning expedition based on a simple idea: inviting students to plan their ideal classroom. Levy's students begin by designing and constructing work desks and raising funds to cover their construction costs by appealing to local investors. Along the way the students discover important lessons about the nature of private property, communal ownership, financial investment, and the economics of starting their own business. The class turns to the story of the Pilgrims as described in William Bradford's diaries to see how some of Europe's first settlers dealt with the problems they faced.

My goal in teaching is to create an environment built on natural inquiry in which students engage in real problems instead of worksheets, original research instead of textbooks; where paper and pencil tests give way to active performances or meaningful products, and excellence is pursued in every detail of our endeavors. I fill my room with a rich variety of activities that allows the genius in each child to be expressed and developed. My class is a tapestry of questions, research, thinking, problem solving, music, poetry, drama, crafts, arts, and games, all integrated in a theme woven anew every year from threads of the children's natural wonder. We often find these themes in common objects in our environment. A grain of wheat, a strand of wool, the shoes we wear, and the name of our town have all led to exciting learning projects. Indeed, I feel a special call to mine the extraordinary out of the everyday. Familiar objects that the children take for granted are filled with intrigue and meaning when we explore their origins. It amazes me that one can start with almost anything, and through a process of questioning, reflecting, and imagining, see through that object, as if it were a window, into the depth and breadth of the world.

Many of our learning adventures had their origin in a question or need of a particular child. Some were planned because I was curious to learn about something myself. Others were inspired by an idea that would bring some life and excitement to a required curriculum subject. Whatever the source of the theme, our curriculum always shares the same basic elements. It starts with a significant question or challenge, then explores sources of answers or expertise, and finally, produces meaningful results that are put in a form that can be shared with others. The fundamental principle is to set learning in the context of reality, where children need to develop knowledge and skills to make decisions or complete tasks relevant to their lives. What follows is a description of one project, which, more than any I have ventured, met my goals for a learning community and the expectations of the Lexington Public Schools.

The Setting

Lexington is a relatively affluent community outside of Boston. The Bowman School, where I teach fourth grade, has approximately 520 students in grades K–5. The challenges of teaching in a suburban community are different from those in an urban or rural setting, but no less formidable. We have a different kind of poverty here than in the city. I call it a poverty of gratitude. The children have many blessings, but they tend to take them for granted and even feel entitled. I have come to believe that a blessing that does not awaken gratitude or compassion actually becomes a curse. It breeds a wasteful and careless attitude toward others and the environment. Thus, one of my biggest challenges in Lexington is to help awaken a sense of gratitude.

One of the ways I do that is by providing opportunities for the children to experience the work it takes on the part of many people to produce the conveniences they have taken for granted. For example, we do a project "From Field to Table," where they see the work it takes to produce a loaf of bread, from planting the wheat, to baking the bread. After they see all the work it takes, buying a loaf of bread from the store is a different experience for these children. We do the same thing in a project "From Fleece to Fabric," where we carry out all the steps in making an article of clothing, from a raw fleece to a piece of knitted or woven fabric. The project I am about to describe, "Pilgrims '92," takes this principle to an extreme.

The Idea

I have attended numerous workshops over the years at which various inspiring experts have described their programs for educational reform. One feature the programs all have in common is that the faculty members are required to spend lots of time together reflecting on what was being taught and what was being learned. I wonder how many of the statistics they cite to support the validity of their programs can really be attributed to the teachers' working together in a reflective way? Give us time to reflect and plan together, and we teachers will make radical improvements in the education of children.

I learned firsthand the transforming power of collaboration when Debbie O'Hara, a tutor in my class, and I went together to a three-day conference. In one of the activities we were asked to design the ideal classroom. Debbie and I went to separate corners of the room to dream, and when we met to share our vision, we were shocked to find that we had independently imagined the same ideal classroom. It was empty. The children would come into an empty classroom and they would design it to meet their learning needs.

We listened at the conference as other groups proposed their ideal environments. We were tempted by the glass door opening into the Japanese gardens. The hot tub in the back of the room was almost too much to resist. But when our turn came, we presented the image of the empty classroom. We described the skills that would be needed to plan, fund, and build a learning environment. The math of designing, measuring, constructing, would offer many challenges. The simple machines that are part of the tools we would use, and the environmental impact of the materials we would consume fit well into our fourth-grade science curriculum. A connection could be made to the Pilgrims, a required fourth-grade social studies unit, who also came to a new environment and had to shape it to meet their needs.

Behind our idea of the empty classroom was a desire to involve the children in the planning that we usually do for them. Sometimes our efforts to organize work space and lessons for our children actually prevent them from experiencing the full measure of pride and joy in creating something out of nothing but their own imagination, perseverance, organization, and effort. We give them coloring books to fill in the lines. We give them worksheets to fill in the blanks. We give them tests to fill in the answers. In this context, the carefully organized room gives them prefabricated spaces and structures to fill in with activities.

An empty classroom seemed like the ultimate blank canvas to put before students. And since we had each thought of this idea independently, we took it as a definite sign that it was to be more than just an exercise at a conference. We felt obliged to try it in September.

The Plan

Once we decided to make it real, we began to think about how we would communicate the value of the project to everyone that would be affected. How would we convince the administration that we could meet the requirements of the Lexington Public Schools? How would we share our idea with the rest of the staff at Bowman School? How would we assure parents that their children would learn all the skills expected of a fourth grader in Lexington?

We made a list of all the kinds of knowledge and skills needed to plan and build a classroom. We outlined the opportunities there would be to develop skills in math, science, reading, writing, social studies, and the arts. We described the physical activities and the challenges we would face in making decisions together as a community.

From this list we produced a document that described in fuller detail the vast opportunities this kind of learning held for the children. We used this plan to demonstrate to the administration and the parents how we would cover the required Lexington curriculum in the context of our expedition. We met with the superintendent, our principal, and our faculty to explain the project and enlist their cooperation. The administration was supportive from the beginning; both the superintendent and the principal were encouraging. But the faculty meeting proved more problematic. Teachers had a variety of responses. Some helped us clarify our vision and adapt our plans. Others were disturbed by the unorthodox approach and how it might compare with their classes. The most strident opposition came from fifth-grade teachers; their objection centered on our hope to stay with the class for two years, which meant one of them would have to switch grades with us the next year. In the end none of them was willing to do that, so it had become a one-year project.

Summer Preparations

That summer, my fifteen-year-old son, who had just finished taking a business course in high school, began chastising me for having kept his money in a regular savings account. He had become aware of the possibilities the stock market offered to improve his rate of return. We began to study the market together, and he invested his savings in several stocks. My investigation of the stock market played a crucial role in how we decided to fund our project. I had previously thought of applying for a grant. But if we supplied the money, I feared we would be robbing the children of the challenge to raise it themselves. These children were too used to having things given to them anyway. What if we offered shares in a corporation? Could we get people in town to invest in our project? Could we establish this program without any money from the school system? We put out a feeler in the local newspaper, a letter to the editor briefly describing our intentions and asking anyone who might be interested in hearing more about the project in the fall to drop us a note. We also sent the letter to a some of businesses and town officials and asked that they send back an enclosure indicating their interest. Eighteen people and businesses wanted to find out more about the project, so there was hope.

We made the final decision to go ahead when we realized the connection to the Pilgrims. To fund their journey to a new world, the Pilgrims got local business to invest in their cause. We would do the same. In fact, we saw a close parallel between our journey and theirs. They came to an unfamiliar world and had to adapt to it and shape it to meet their needs. We would come into an empty classroom and do the same. The Pilgrims could be our model. Whenever we came to a problem, we would research whether the Pilgrims ever confronted the same issue and whether or not their course of action could inform our decision. Looking back at Pilgrim life became a refrain throughout the year. William Bradford's diary served as our primary resource about how some of our country's first European settlers dealt with some of the same problems we faced in our classroom challenge. We would call ourselves "Pilgrims '92."

Of course, the Pilgrims encountered an existing people and culture when they arrived. The Native American experience, the focus of more in-depth study at another grade level in Lexington, was not a focal point of our project, though we did set the Pilgrims' journey in its broader historical context. Without glorifying the Pilgrim culture, we studied its strengths and weaknesses in the context of the physical challenges and inner dynamics of people trying to build a community.

Once the project was definite, we met with parents whose children would be in the class. We wanted to make sure they supported the idea and to give those who did not approve an opportunity to switch their child into a different fourth-grade class. One family had concerns about the capitalist overtones they sensed in our written plan. It took us two meetings to work through the difficulties. We saw it was important to stress the idea of a *cooperative* rather than a corporation, and in the end, this proved to be an important distinction. These parents were to be among our most enthusiastic supporters.

Finally, we sent a letter to the children over the summer and asked them to draw a map of their ideal classroom and bring it to school on the first day. When they arrived in Room 9 in September, they found an empty classroom.

The Year Begins

The first day of school, after expressing our initial amazement at the empty classroom, we settled into a circle and began to discuss what we were going to do. We shared our maps and began to plan how to meet the challenge of creating a learning environment with no resources but our own wits and effort.

We needed some supplies, and our first issue was getting some pencils for writing. We talked about where we should keep our pencils and the question arose, "Should we each have our own pencil, or should we own them collectively, keeping them in a common location and taking them when we need them?" The debate was lively. Over the next two weeks the students tried owning them in common, but it wasn't long before the last one to the cup found no pencils left. It was not much longer before the last five found no pencils. Then people began holding on to the pencils rather than putting them back. We tried private ownership. It was better until arguments broke out.

"Hey, that's my pencil."

"No way! It's definitely mine."

The advantages and disadvantages of common and private ownership were clear. What did the Pilgrims do?

We were amazed to read in William Bradford's diary that in the early years of the Plymouth Plantation everything was owned in common. The food a family grew went into the common store. People took out according to need. The clothes the women sewed went into the common store. There was no private property. Then Bradford wrote that the community was in a terrible crisis of production. They did not have enough food. Morale was low. A town meeting was held, and it was decided to give each family its own property. Suddenly production dramatically increased. Women, who before this time had never worked on the farm, joined their husbands and children in the fields from morning until night. But what about the poor widows or sick who couldn't work? Must they starve in a private economy? A certain portion was taken from each family and used to help those in need. "Does that remind you of something today?" I asked. "Taxes!" cried Lillian. Sure enough, we work and get money for our labor. But we each give a portion of our earnings to the "common store" to meet our joint concerns and to help those who are in need.

So our first problem of how to manage our pencils led us into fascinating discussions of socialism, private ownership, and the concept of taxes for the common good. I am often amazed at the children's ability to understand deep and complex issues when they can relate these issues to something in their own experience. Emerson wrote, "The student interprets the age of chivalry by his own age of chivalry, and the days of maritime adventure by quite parallel miniature experiences of his own. To the sacred history of the world he has the same key."[1] Through the lens of their own experience with their pencils, the children were able to begin to understand complex issues of modern economy and government.

While we were settling our pencil dilemma, our attention was focused on the maps of the ideal classroom that the children had brought to school. Although the children's designs for the room were very interesting, all had one thing in common: they assumed that there was ample space to fit anything in—desks, tables, work areas, and meeting areas, with room to spare. One child even had space for a swimming pool! It was clear the first activity would be to redraw the maps according to scale. This wasn't part of our plan, but the need was obvious and the time was ripe.

Scale is a fascinating concept. You can fit the whole world on a single piece of paper. We used careful measurement, multiplication, division, fractions, and ratios to reconstruct our maps according to scale. Each child then presented his or her scale design to the class.

The Cooperative: Involving the Community

As we compared our ideas for the classroom, our next task became clear. We had to decide what kind of work surfaces we wanted and whether we would build or buy them. The students were quick to agree on building them. I had imagined we would sit at tables for four or six, thinking fewer, larger pieces would be more manageable. But the students were passionate about having their own desks. I believe I should always try to help them accomplish their vision, but I could not imagine building twenty-three desks, and I don't like to take on a project I don't think we can achieve with high standards. I tried to convince them that the time and expense of building twenty-three individual desks would be prohibitive. They were willing to strike a compromise: we would make twelve two-person desks.

"Where are you going to get the wood? The tools?" I challenged. "You will need some money to begin. How will you get it?"

The Pilgrims provided the model. How did they finance their voyage? We read about the investment agreement between the Pilgrims and the "Merchants and Adventurers in London" in Bradford's diary. We talked about how investments were different from donations. An investor expects something back, a dividend. Did we have anything to give back to our community? The children had many ideas, from various direct services to products from our class projects: a loaf of bread from winter wheat we would grow, harvest, process, and bake; a weaving from wool we would wash, card, spin, dye, and weave; a weekly newsletter to report our progress and activities; invitations to seasonal performances of music, poetry, dance, and drama; calendars from a project in geometric construction. Finally, an investor also expects to receive the principal back, and better yet a profit, when the project is complete. We thought we could sell our assets at the end of the year to raise funds to return the investments.

But first we needed to identify local businesses or individuals who might be interested in purchasing a share. Those who had indicated interest during the summer were our first contacts. All the places in town the children frequented—restaurants, drug stores, toy stores—were also candidates. Combing the Yellow Pages yielded an extensive list of potential investors. Individuals were also allowed to invest, providing they did not have any children in the school. We wanted to involve people who would not ordinarily have any contact with the school so they could see some of the positive things happening in education. The children wrote letters to all the potential investors, enticing them with dividends, and inviting them to purchase a share in our cooperative for $50. We hoped to sell twenty shares to raise $1,000.

There is nothing quite like the excitement of receiving mail in class, especially when you open it and find checks from investors. Sixteen businesses bought shares, including three banks, the neighborhood ice cream store, a hardware store, a softball team, a craft store, a Realtor, a car dealer, and a restaurant. Eighteen individuals (including a member of the Board of Selectmen) joined the cooperative; some of them were senior citizens. These thirty-four shareholders bought a total of forty-three shares. (There were other people who wanted to invest, but we were worried about being able to produce dividends for so many members, so we closed the offering. We did invite various community friends to join as honorary members.)

We had $2,075 in checks. What should we do with the money? The children wanted to put it in the bank, but which bank? We invited representatives from the three banks who invested to explain why we should deposit our money in their institutions. One offered a higher interest rate, but would charge one dollar for every transaction. Another offered lower interest, but a free account. The children had to figure out which was the best offer. They learned how interest worked and estimated the number of transactions we would conduct. They decided on the bank that offered the free account.

One of the investors was an accountant, so we invited her in to teach us how to set up the books and keep careful records of our financial activities. The accounting throughout the year offered rich opportunities to learn and practice our math skills. We calculated our finances weekly, and issued quarterly statements for the investors.

Building the Desks

Now we returned to the furniture design. One of our shareholders, Mr. Cassell, was a craftsman, so we invited him to our class to discuss our furniture needs and help us develop a design for our desks. We determined how big the surface area needed to be for two people to work comfortably. We wanted a design that would allow us to flip the top of the desks vertically so we could store them against the wall when we needed open space in the classroom. Mr. Cassell showed us designs for desks that might have been used by the Pilgrims. We chose a design and Mr. Cassell built us a scale model. We constructed a prototype, proposed some modifications, and finalized a design. We decided to use hand tools and pegs for construction, because that's the way the Pilgrims would have done it. The students would build the desks (and later the chairs) during the project time (an hour at the end of the day) and any free time (before school, after school, and during recess).

Planning, buying, and cutting the wood offered many real-life mathematical challenges. For example, our desk tops were to measure three feet by four feet. Plywood comes in 4-foot-by-8-foot sheets. How many sheets do we need to build twelve desks? How will we cut the wood so as to have the least amount of waste, and the most useful shapes left over for use in another project? Two-by-fours come in lengths of 6, 8, 10, 12, 14, or 16 feet. We want to cut feet for the desk legs that are eighteen inches long. What length of two-by-four can be cut into 18-inch sections without any waste?

Problems like these are always more motivating and interesting than abstract ones from a book. The children are motivated because getting the right answer really counts. Real business transactions will be undertaken based on their calculations. Problems like this also have more than one possible solution. For example, in the plywood problem most of the children figured out that we could cut five 2-foot-by-3-foot pieces from each sheet of plywood. Theodore's answer was four pieces from each, so I called him over to my desk to show him how he could cut a fifth piece if he rotated the board. He said, "Yeah, I saw that, but I figured whether you cut four or five pieces, you will still need three sheets of plywood for twelve desks. By cutting only four tops from each sheet, you will have larger and more useful pieces left over." To solve the two-by-four problem, the children cut paper models of the different lengths to scale and cut them in pieces to see which could be cut evenly. They worked with great precision, because their own money was at stake.

Staining the wood offered another great mathematical challenge. After we had constructed the desks, we had to figure out how much stain we needed to buy to finish them. The class worked in small groups measuring the surface area of the desks, which included: rectangles, trapezoids, and cylinders. They had to measure tops, bottoms, and edges because the whole thing would be stained. They had to translate square inches to square feet (not by dividing by twelve, as many of them thought!). I gave them brochures telling how many square feet would be covered by a pint, quart, or gallon of stain. One group, in an attempt to be as thrifty as possible, figured we needed one gallon, one quart, and one pint. They were shocked to find the cost of their proposal would be considerably more than another group's recommendation of two gallons. A great lesson in the economy of purchasing in quantity!

Rhythm of the Day

I ordered the school day so that my students did the work most intellectually demanding in the morning and most physically active the last thing in the afternoon. The day was divided into four main parts. We began each morning with music and poetry recitation as a segue into a ninety-minute period I called *theme time*. We focused on the analytical and creative aspects of the project during theme time—thinking, planning, writing, reviewing, researching, making decisions. Theme time was interdisciplinary; the work might be focused on different subjects depending on the present need. The second half of the morning was reserved for skills. If I noticed that the children did not know the proper form for writing letters to the investors, I taught them this skill. If we had to make a decision about which bank to put our money in and I saw that they didn't understand interest, I explained it and gave them an opportunity to explore it and apply the concept in other situations. If they needed to learn skills, primarily in math and language arts, that did not relate directly to the project, we practiced them then. (Children receiving extra help outside the classroom received it during skill time, not theme time.) After lunch we had a fourth five-minute reading time. Sometimes the literature related to the theme, but more often it did not. Then the last hour and fifteen minutes was hands-on time. Different groups of children worked on different things. Some built desks, others wrote the newsletter, still others worked with wool or wheat, figuring out how it gets from raw form to finished product.

Consensus

We made all our decisions by consensus. We sat in a circle on the floor, and each person had a chance to state an opinion or pass. After all opinions had been heard, students were invited to defend their ideas or to explain how their opinions had been modified by what they heard from their classmates. Most discussions were very civil, and consensus was clear. Sometimes, the discussions were more passionate, and it took longer to make a decision. This was often the case when I proposed spending our funds to buy things. I was not reluctant to spend our money, thinking that we could sell our assets at the end of the year and get it back. But the children never wanted to spend money on something they could get in some other way. Instead of our buying tools, those who could brought in tools from home. When we needed a vacuum cleaner (so we could clean up our own considerable messes and not provoke our custodian), they made an appeal through the newsletter and got one donated.

The only time the children wanted to spend our money was to help someone in need, and then they were extravagant. Once we read that people in Mali had been forced to eat their seed crop because of famine. UNICEF offered a program through which one could buy seeds for the people of Mali. Each package had enough seeds to sustain a whole village. One package contained common grains, another particular seeds unique to the African climate. Should we send the common grains or the African ones? After much debate, the children were still divided. Then one child said, "Let's send them one of each!" Everyone cheered. Another said, "Let's send *two* of each!" More cheers. We also sent them a bag of seeds harvested from our own wheat garden.

Another time we read in the newspaper that a teacher in Boston who used music extensively in his kindergarten class had had his keyboard and tape recorder stolen. The children found the telephone number of the school where the teacher taught, called him, and offered to send money to replace the equipment. In return they asked for a tape of his children singing.

The class community is forged as we learn to reconcile individual differences. Learning when to set aside our own opinion for the sake of the group and when to fight for what we believe in is a discernment we refine all of our lives. Sometimes decisions were held up because people felt strongly about their point of view. It was especially exciting when, in the midst of ponderous debate, someone would have an idea that would break the stalemate. For example, we had to design a stock certificate for our shareholders. One of the members was a stockbroker, so we invited him in to show us what certificates looked like. He brought in the certificates of various companies (the New England Patriots certificate made a big hit) and we learned what all the numbers and symbols represented. Then each child designed his or her own for Pilgrim '92. A committee was formed to take the best elements from all the designs and incorporate them into a certificate. While the group was working, another child designed a beautiful and very official-looking certificate on the computer. His design sparked one of the most serious debates of the year: which to use, the hand-drawn one or the computer creation?

Most of the children thought the investors would prefer the computer design because it looked so official. But there was an unyielding lobbying for the hand-drawn one. It represented many hours of hard work, and besides, the Pilgrims would never have used a computer. The few who preferred the hand-drawn certificate felt too strongly to give in. I couldn't see how we were going to find consensus and was about to call for a vote, when one of the children suggested we print the certificate on thick stock, with the hand-drawn version on one side and the computer image on the other. Fantastic! I told them how corporations use proxies to solicit the opinions of their shareholders. We sent the two-sided certificate to each shareholder, along with a proxy asking them which side they intended to display. We also used the proxy for some market research to determine the value of a completed desk for accounting purposes. As I had hoped, almost all the shareholders said they liked the hand-drawn side better. This was a valuable lesson to the children. Even though something that uses the latest technology may look more polished and professional, the handmade product is much more valuable.

The Desk Olympics

When the desks were finally constructed, we celebrated with a ceremony that lasted all day. In the morning we sang songs that had been written for the occasion and recited poems and stories about the desks. Special songs honored Mr. Cassell, our craftsman, and Mr. Ritchie, a retired citizen who came in many afternoons to help the children build. Dances demonstrated movements of the tools we used in construction. Finally, in a long-anticipated moment, we all sat down together for the first time.

The afternoon was given over to the "Desk Olympics." The children invented many contests involving the desks—high jumps over, limbo under—and other classroom challenges.

The Auction

At the end of the year we invited the shareholders and parents to a celebration with dinner, closing ceremonies, and an auction. The children recited a class poem they had written about the year. But the most exciting part of the evening was the auction. One of the principles of investing is that the investors have the right at any time to sell their shares and receive their portion of the assets. At the beginning of the year we had promised the shareholders that we would return their investment to them at the end of the year. We planned to do this by liquidating all our assets.

We had also studied how the value of something was determined by the law of supply and demand, so throughout the year we had a little "museum" of items of value to the citizens of Room 9. These included the confetti gathered from the holes we punched in binding our geometric calendars; some wheat seeds left over from our wheat harvest; some wool left over from our weaving project; knitting needles we made from wooden dowels; a framed leaf, the last one hanging on the oak tree outside our window, a tree we'd written about all year. We put these items on the auction block. Children took turns being the auctioneer, and by the end of the night they could rattle off the customary "I've got five, who'll give me ten?" with the best of them.

We'd raffled off one desk to someone in the school; another to someone in our class. After three of the remaining desks were sold to the highest bidders at the auction, we'd raised enough money to pay back all the investors. That meant we still had seven desks. We could have sold them and made a handsome (100 percent) profit for the shareholders. But the shareholders voted to return them to the class. Six were taken home by children chosen by lot, and the seventh desk remains in my classroom as a monument to the momentous voyage of Pilgrims '92.

Beyond the obvious benefits of the financial support, our partnership with the community gave the children a tremendous sense of motivation to excel in their work. Learning was released from the confines of the classroom, and children were set free to explore the world. The partnership gave the children something their parents and teachers could never provide. Children *expect* parents and teachers to be interested in their activities. But the interest from the businesses and citizens of our community was completely unexpected. It inspired our gratitude and motivated us to work hard in everything we did. It also gave the community a firsthand glimpse of what is happening in our schools and opened up possibilities for future involvement. In fact, one of our investors went on to join our site-based council. At the end of the year, when we attempted to return the investments to the shareholders, most of them asked us to keep the funds for a new project the following year. But that's another story.

Making History While We Study It

Throughout the whole year, we were aware that we were making history at the same time we studied it. We were able to learn about the Pilgrims because William Bradford had written a diary. How would people three hundred years from today know anything about what our lives were like? The weekly newsletters were one way we reflected and reported on our story. But unlike the Pilgrims, we also had technology that could record images to show future generations what our lives were like. We decided to make a video with the help of an extraordinarily dedicated and talented parent, who videotaped throughout the year and took groups of children to the high school to help her edit. The children wrote the script.[2]

Reflections

The following year, students, parents, and other teachers walked by my classroom in September, astonished to see traditional desks set in rows. "Mr. Levy's room with desks in rows?!" they exclaimed. I tried to explain that the desks didn't really matter. It doesn't have anything to do with how you arrange your desks or how you design your room. What really counts is the relationship between the teacher and the class, the kind of community that is forged between people. The reason I feel confident to undertake such bold activities with such unknown outcomes is that I know my relationship with the children and the quality of the community we will build together will be strong enough to overcome any obstacle.

"But won't you do this project again?" they inquired. No, I suspect not. For one thing, a project like this requires a tremendous amount of help from many other people. I would hesitate to ask them all to do it again. Their help came freely and with joy the first time, and I would hate to risk seeing it become an obligation. On a more personal note, I would not do it again for the same reason an artist would not paint the same picture again, or a musician would not compose the same piece of music again. Teaching is an art. A project like this is better framed as a unique creation of all the individuals who worked to make it happen: students, teachers, parents, and community members. Each year brings together a new configuration of people with a unique calling, unlike any that has gone before. I listen for it every year.

---

[1] Ralph Waldo Emerson, "History," in *The Portable Emerson*, ed. Mark Van Doren (New York: Viking 1946), p. 155.

[2] Video is available: write to Steven Levy at 11 Fletcher Avenue, Lexington, MA 02173.

5

Learning Noise

Vivian Stephens with Meg Campbell

In this chapter, Vivian Stephens, a twenty-year veteran, reflects on her evolution as a teacher. Stephens describes the challenges of shedding familiar but less effective teaching strategies and assimilating new ways of thinking about her practice. Stephens's view of herself as a learner inspires a searching interest in her own professional growth which leads her to look critically at her practice, and to seek out professional development opportunities that challenge some of her most closely held beliefs. Stephens's story tells us that the ambiguity and uncertainty that come with making sense of new practice are at the heart of constructing a personal knowledge-base that guides teaching. In particular, Stephens's professional knowledge grows in areas that touch on the learning of learners, classroom management, subject matter, and instructional strategies.

Beginnings

I am a child at heart. Chronologically I am forty-six years old, but I don't feel it. I feel ten, like my children. I dash here and there. If my students can do it, I can do it, including running, jumping rope, and playing ball. I'm growing as my students grow. I can still learn. I still want to learn.

I am the fifth of nine children and the first one to finish college. I grew up in the country near a small rural town called Irwington, Georgia. My father was a wonderful man who loved to harvest the earth. He grew cotton, watermelons, peanuts, and corn. My mother stayed home to raise her children. She had taught in a one-room schoolhouse when she was younger at a time in the South when teaching was one of the few occupations available to African-American women. To this day, my mother has a great love of poetry and literature, and well-developed oratory skills. She saw to it that each of her nine children could recite an author from memory—Paul Laurence Dunbar and Henry Wadsworth Longfellow are her favorites.

I hated to miss school, but at certain times of the year I had to stay at home and help with the harvest. Every morning I rode an old school bus to a poor, consolidated elementary and high school. This was in the days before integration, so most of our books were given to us from the white school in town. Needless to say, by the time we got them they were in pretty poor condition. But that didn't prevent our teachers from selling ice cream and snacks during recess to buy us books and other resources. I was very fortunate to have teachers who saw more in me than I saw in myself. Once I decided to teach, I wanted to do the same for my own students.

I always knew that college was in my future. Growing up in the rural South, it didn't take me long to realize that getting a good education could open doors for me that had been shut tight for Southern African-American women of my mother's generation. At a young age I decided it was important to me to be able to support myself and never be financially dependent on anyone else. For me as a woman, college was one way I could do that.

My first major in college was vocational home economics. I wanted to be a buyer for a department store, but I soon learned that this didn't fit my personality. When I thought about what might be a better profession for me, I drew on the memory of a wonderful social studies teacher of mine named Robert James. Mr. James was a mentor for me. I was his assistant, and he often trusted me by giving me what seemed to my young mind to be extremely important responsibilities, like staying after school and entering grades in his grade books. When I thought about Mr. James, my mother, and all the other teachers who had had such a big impact in my life, I knew I wanted to teach.

I began teaching the way I was taught. My elementary teachers mostly lectured to us, and we read from basal readers. We rarely did projects. Every now and then my teachers might bring something into class—a flower cutting, for instance—but we would never dissect it or learn the scientific names for the parts of the flower, as I do now with my students.

If you had walked into my classroom during my first few years as a teacher, you would have seen children sitting in perfect rows. There might have been one or two children stuck in a corner because of behavior problems. But other than that you would have seen row after row. There would have been very little in the way of group activity. Instead, it was "Read chapter six, and answer questions one through five." My curriculum was organized around workbooks.

The first three years I taught in this way. Then I transferred to another school where there were teachers who taught reading and math in an innovative way. Working with these teachers and seeing up close their openness to new approaches began to influence me. I couldn't stand to see a teacher doing new things in her classroom that I didn't know about. One of those innovative people was the librarian, Judy Greene, who is now my principal at Clairemont Elementary. Judy has a gift for helping others grow. She's always been able to see abilities in people they can't see in themselves. She's never been one to push, but she always encourages. She always says, "Vivian, you can do it!" In turn, I try to do that for my children because I know there are some children who feel they just can't achieve, when I know they can.

As librarian, Judy would wheel her cart stacked high with books into our classroom for a book talk. She made it a habit to read every new book that came to the library. Children would say, "Oh, save that one for me." And she would. Out of all those hundreds of students, how she kept track of which child wanted which book I will never know. She has that kind of mind.

One of my first contacts with Judy was when I went to her with a problem. My children hated writing book reports in a rigid format, and I wondered if it might help them if they had someone to talk to about their books, someone who was herself an avid reader. So I asked Judy if my children could come and talk with her and she could ask them questions about what they'd read and what they'd written about what they'd read. So every morning a few of my students would write down the title and author of the book they were reading on a list we kept and they'd go to see Judy. (Later, I discovered the value of providing children with different opportunities to discuss what they're reading with their peers. But this insight was still a few years away.) We started keeping a list of books the children had read, and over time it grew. Almost 100 percent of our students were African American, and most of them were quite poor, but their reading scores began to skyrocket. Each student was reading at least one book a week, which was above the norm for their grade level. This was a simple idea, but it worked. It was a way of encouraging children to practice, and Judy was right there to support them.

About fifteen years ago, I began using literature as the basis of my reading program, in large part because it was a way I could focus on character development in my students. The prevailing culture in the school where I taught was that whenever there was a new student, he or she was forced into a fight as a part of an initiation rite. So I read *The Eighteenth Emergency,* by Betsy Byars, with my students because it told the story of what it felt like to be bullied and dishonored. Stories like these have the power to give children a different way of thinking about their behavior and the choices they make. Since then, the stories I choose often have some

kind of moral. They help children learn about ethical issues through looking at someone else's life. I ask my students to generate ideas of how they
can help a character who's faced with a particular moral dilemma. What
should this character have done? Was there a better way to have solved his
problem rather than fighting? What could he have done to restore this child's
honor? I like them to discuss issues like these with each other, not just me.
We come up with questions about a text, and they go off in pairs to talk
them over. Then we come back together and dig a little deeper.

Learning Noise

Before my involvement with Expeditionary Learning, my children didn't
sit in clusters as they do now. There were no class meetings. They didn't
write in their journals as they do now. I didn't build time for reflection into
the day. Aside from a literature-based reading program, I relied on workbooks. My lesson plans were fairly traditional. I had a few hands-on activities that helped children learn content, but by and large students filled
out a lot of worksheets. Children took home stacks of them. I had a hard
time keeping track of them all. When we did a project, which was rare, it
was often science related. It was usually an experiment out of a book which
they took home and practiced. Then they'd come back to class the next
day and perform it. We never sustained a focus on a particular area of
science.

Moving to a project-based approach was hard for me, not the least of
which was the noise level. When I was a young student, children were not
supposed to talk in school. A good classroom meant a silent classroom where
children worked individually at their desks. You used to be able to hear a pin
drop in my classroom. Children had to be absolutely quiet. There was little
give and take. If there was noise, that meant the children must be off-task.
Now learning noise is something I invite into my classroom. Projects *are* noisy.
But it's that good kind of noise. It's learning noise. It's purposeful. It's not the
kind of noise that comes from fighting or behavioral problems. It's working
noise. Working noise is necessary. When teachers work together they're noisy,
so why shouldn't there be noise when children work together? Sure, it was
scary at first. I found myself justifying the noise to anyone who visited my
classroom. I felt I needed to explain what was going on because if someone
didn't know what to look for, he or she might misunderstand and not see that
learning was taking place.

For me, teaching now means listening to students ideas and helping
them pursue those ideas. It means letting them start something and see for
themselves that it won't work. This way children learn to find information

and follow *their own* questions rather than answering questions at the end of the chapter. It's learning that stays with them.

Through my work with Expeditionary Learning, I am better able to involve my students in making decisions that affect their learning. Last year I assessed my students' reading abilities, and I came up with a list of skills that I felt they needed help with. I challenged my students to come up with a way for all of us to learn them. They generated three options. The first idea was for me to teach the students who needed help in small groups, while those who had mastered the skills would read on their own. Their second alternative was that I would teach the skills to the entire class, including those students who already knew them. In other words, they would all learn them again together. The third option was for those who knew a particular skill to coach—they used the word *teach*—those who didn't know it.

When they settled on the last option my mouth fell open. I think they chose this approach because they had started trusting each other so that nobody was afraid to show his or her weaknesses and ask for help. That moment was a beautiful outgrowth of the team building we'd been doing. But their decision challenged my practice, because at first it made me feel they could do without me; I didn't feel needed. I felt like a fish out of water. Soon, however, I realized that I was still needed, but that their choice had forced me to change roles. I had to relinquish the role of teacher that I'd become comfortable with and, in effect, help *them* become the teachers. Their decision forced me to pull together materials quickly for the "teachers" to use with their "students." It was like preparing for ten classes. I gave the materials I had prepared to the teams of students and teachers. But before the teachers sat down with their students they reviewed the materials on their own. They devised their own plans and strategies for teaching. They also designed games and activities that went beyond the materials I had provided them. They only came to me if they had a problem.

We often set aside a special time we call "reflection time," where we reflect as a group on a shared learning experience we have just had. During class reflection time the students who were "reading teachers" shared their frustration in trying to get an idea across, and the elation they felt when their students finally understood. The students talked about how comfortable they felt with the whole process. After listening to them talk, I was convinced that I was doing the right thing. I have to admit, when I saw what capable peer tutors they were, it was a revelation. Since then, I've often used this approach. Now children make many of the decisions in my class. It takes some of the emphasis off my coming up with highly detailed lesson plans. But it means I have to work harder at listening to children and then using what I learn to direct their learning. I'm always amazed at what children can do, how much they want to learn, and how much more detailed and thoughtful their work can be when they have the opportunity to pursue it in depth.

Teacher Learning

I never would have dreamed of designing a house, nor did I know I'd even be interested in it. But several summers ago I went on an Expeditionary Learning professional development "summit" for educators—a kind of learning expedition for teachers. I signed up thinking I would learn about styles of architecture. But much to my surprise that's not what I got. Instead, we were immersed day and night in learning the technical skills we'd need to design a new home. We could be as creative as we wanted to be. Our final project was to draw extremely detailed blueprints using all the skills we'd learned. Once it was over I asked myself, "I've spent a week of my life doing this. Now, how can I pull it together so that my fourth graders can do it?" I knew I couldn't replicate the exact expedition with my fourth graders, but I felt I could build on what I had learned.

The message I received during the summit was that it was all right not to know all the answers. If I had had to know everything before taking the first step in teaching this expedition, I would never have undertaken it. This was a very new experience for me. I can remember times when students would ask me questions that I didn't have the answer for and I would feel like a complete idiot. I was the teacher, after all, so I was supposed to have all the answers. I grew up with that conception of teaching. Sometimes when I'm teaching my children I find myself in the dark. I have to tell them, "I'm learning just like you." When they come to me about something I don't understand, I tell them, "I don't know. Let's go find out." I'm very comfortable with saying this, but I wasn't always.

Back at Clairemont Elementary, I designed an architecture expedition that drew from my summit experience. We toured homes in Inman Park, which was Atlanta's first suburb, built at the turn of the century in Victorian style. We studied architecturally interesting houses in Decatur and examined their exterior features. We studied floor plans from different kinds of dwellings. My students often came into school saying, "My mom didn't know what a turret is!" They loved learning things their parents did not know. They were perfectly content to turn their desks into drafting tables, which is what we did. They often had to work on the floor because their desks were covered with drafts of their blueprints. We also had architects come in. It was reassuring to know that there were professionals from our community whom I could draw on for advice. It put me in a different role—from having to know all the answers to being a facilitator and organizer.

The architecture expedition taught me that a good project is something that children can get their hands on, something they actually build or make, and one that improves after critique and revision. If a student can produce his or her best work on the first try, the assignment is not challenging enough.

My experience as a learner in the architecture summit influenced my own teaching practice in two other important and lasting ways. In the summit, we had class meetings every day where we could talk things out in a thoughtful, safe way. We also critiqued each other's work and outside experts—in this case, professional architects—offered their candid views on where our work needed improvement. Before that professional development experience, I had never had daily class meetings or critique sessions of student work in progress. The two practices support each other.

Peer Critique

I had always asked students to share their work, but I didn't have them critique each other in the way they do now. It was more negative than positive feedback. I borrowed the idea from the architecture summit, where we would critique each other's blueprints, first offering positive comments about the strengths of the work. Then we would get into what could be improved; what were the areas for growth. The architecture summit provided me with not just the strategy of critique, but the words for describing it. Having a language for critique helps me to understand it and communicate it to children better. When we talk in my class about being kind, they know that they need to start with something positive before they move into areas of improvement. I have the author sit on an "author's stool" in front of the room, and everyone gathers around on the carpet. It's like saying, "It's time for you to listen to me." When the author has finished, she calls on her peers for their feedback.

For me, peer critique is built on the strength of relationship in this class—how we treat one another. This is nowhere clearer than in the case of struggling students like Shante. This is my second year with Shante because she's repeating the fourth grade this year, and I'm really concerned that she not fall between the cracks. She's doing well right now, but I'm worried about her moving on next year. One of the things that has really helped her to turn the corner is her comfort level with the class. But I'm worried that once she leaves here she might crawl back into her shell. She has a lot of insecurities that come from being a slow learner, and I think that her attitude toward her work very much depends on the situation she's in.

Last year Shante rarely raised her hand to ask a question. She associated only with a small segment of her classmates. She couldn't write coherent sentences. She had difficulty reading and comprehending on a third-grade level and almost never felt comfortable about sharing her writing. She rarely participated in group activities. She was a classic passive learner. Now, thanks to the support she gets from her peers, she's a good deal less inhibited when it comes to expressing an opinion and getting actively engaged in her learning. She'll volunteer to be a group leader. She no longer chooses to work only with children of her same race. She doesn't concede an argument just because she thinks someone else may know more about an issue than she does. Instead she tends to push for understanding by trying to clarify things for herself.

The other day Shante did an oral report that I think indicates her new outlook on her work. I don't allow my students to stand up and read aloud their reports, so they're forced to practice a lot before they get in front of the class. Shante rose to the occasion. She had put together a report on elephant herds and shared with the class what she'd learned. Her classmates sat spellbound. When she finished the classroom erupted into applause. This is a far cry from how she used to approach her presentations. Shante used to flounder quite a bit. There was no continuity, no flow, no organization in her presentations. She couldn't remember what she wanted to say. Many times she wouldn't even finish a project, so there was nothing for her to present. Now there's a willingness to attack the work.

The critiquing that followed her presentation was very positive, and she was able to answer almost all queries. She doesn't seem to feel she has to pretend that she knows something when she doesn't. She allows her weak areas to show. She asks questions. She admits when she doesn't understand something. She asks for clarification—from both me and her classmates. Last year, she wouldn't ask questions because she didn't want her classmates to know she didn't understand. I think there was a fear of being ridiculed because of what she didn't know. One of the things that has helped her is the way my students critique each other's work, especially their oral presentations. They look for the good points first. Then they make suggestions about how they can improve and what might be missing. Everyone has to go through the critiquing process. No one is exempt. It's a chance to talk about things we're good at and those we have to work on. Now we recognize that when we make mistakes those are areas for growth, and we all have them.

My children are spirited, rambunctious in September when they come in. Sometimes they can also be disrespectful to each other. But after our time together, they leave here caring about each other. My children keep me inspired and wanting to improve as a teacher. I'm a restless kind of learner, especially when it comes to looking for ways to get better at what I do. The children also challenge me to listen for my own "learning noise." It's not hard to hear.

Brother, Can You Spare a Dime? Designing a Learning Expedition on the Great Depression

Christine Cziko

In this chapter, Christine Cziko (formerly a humanities teacher at School for the Physical City in New York) describes how she and her teacher-colleague, Betsy McGee designed a learning expedition on the social, political, and economic issues of the Depression era. Cziko walks us through the delicate process of conceptualizing their expedition, including its learning goals, how it unfolds in the classroom and the streets of New York City, and the adjustments they make along the way to accommodate students' ideas and interests. A challenge for Cziko is balancing her rigorous learning goals with her students' varying abilities by providing multiple strategies for students to find their own way into the subject matter.

As a member of the founding faculty of the School for the Physical City and an English teacher with more than twenty years of experience, I was both exhilarated and terrified at the prospect of helping to create a new school. Having worked with the New York City Writing Project for many years, I felt confident in my ability to create a classroom environment in which students could use both reading and writing as tools for thinking and learning. But I had never designed extended, interdisciplinary, hands-on learning projects, and I struggled to understand what was really meant by "Expeditionary Learning."

Designing an expedition seemed daunting. As I understood it, there was a kind of open-endedness to the process that left me feeling uneasy. The truth was that I did not really understand what an expedition was or how to begin one, and so I began by reading about the learning expeditions other teachers had designed. Although I found the descriptions fascinating, most of these expeditions had been designed by elementary school teachers whose teaching situations differed from my own in significant ways.

First, I did not have the kind of extended, all-day time with my students that was common in elementary school settings. Although classes were not limited to forty-five-minute periods and the staff could build in some flexible scheduling, like weekly "team days" for out-of-school trips and activities, students still went to different classes for math, science, history, and English.

Second, I did not have complete freedom regarding curriculum choices. Even in ninth grade, high school teachers feel the pressure to begin preparing their students to face the battery of subject area tests they must pass in order to get a high school diploma in the state of New York. Content counts, and any expedition we planned had to engage students while meeting the expectations held by our school for high school work.

Finally, most of the expeditions I read about were based on math or science themes. I am an English teacher, and one of my primary goals is to help students become competent and committed readers and writers. What does it mean, I asked myself, to make reading and writing "expeditionary"?

Meanwhile, school had started, and I found myself basically doing in my classroom what I knew how to do: creating a place where my ninth-grade students could read, respond to, discuss, and share literature they cared about, while also exploring and writing on themes in their own lives. There was certainly learning going on—but was it "expeditionary," and did that really matter?

Conceptualizing the Expedition

It was November when I began having long conversations with my colleague Betsey McGee, the ninth-grade history teacher. We decided to design an interdisciplinary expedition on the Great Depression, focusing on the year 1934 and, in particular, on what was happening at that time in New York City. Meanwhile, in our new school we were just beginning to get over the shock of our inadequate space (two classrooms, divided by a closing wall that never really closed), lack of materials (we still had not received books that had been ordered in July), and the general chaos that is part of starting a new school ("Who has the keys to the bathroom?"). More important, we were beginning to know our students and had a clear sense of both their strengths and their needs. We had to design an expedition that would support our struggling learners while challenging our more competent learners. This meant careful planning, so we decided to give ourselves two months' lead time. Our goal was to begin the expedition after winter vacation.

Looking back on how we ultimately created this expedition, I can see three distinct, though overlapping, stages to our work: conceptualizing, designing, and delivering the learning expedition. Simply put—thinking, planning, and doing. Though we learned much from looking back and thinking about what we had actually done, Betsey and I were, from the start, very purposeful in our design of this expedition. We wanted to be clear about both what we were doing and why.

In our early conversations, Betsey and I struggled with our goals for this learning expedition. During the initial planning phase of our school, the faculty at SPC identified and committed itself to three types of learning goals: community- and character-building goals, learning-to-be-a-learner goals, and content goals. We wanted this expedition to reflect and help students achieve these goals.

Community and Character Building

First, we at SPC believe that we have the responsibility to help students develop as whole people with both individual integrity and a sense of responsibility to their community. Betsey and I felt that both community- and character-building goals had to be central to this expedition. We set about to design "guiding questions"—questions that would raise both the personal and the public issues that faced Americans in the 1930s. We asked ourselves which questions would be meaningful and engaging to students, as well as significant and central to an understanding of the Depression.

As the historian, Betsey spent some time trying to articulate a crucial "community-building" question raised by the Depression. She settled on the following: What conditions (economic and political) are necessary for a democracy to thrive? During the 1930s, democracy was endangered, not only in the United States, but around the world. In Europe, many countries fell to fascism and dictatorship. She asked: What conditions threaten democracy? What can we learn from the thirties about how to safeguard democracy today?

Taking on the character-building goal, and building on the reading and writing my students had done about decision making in the first part of the term, I came up with these questions: What choices do people have when faced with inequality and adversity? What are the strategies people use in the face of hardship? In the 1930s people responded to the Depression in many different ways. Some just tried to work harder, while others turned to crime. There were those who attempted to escape the harsh realities they faced through excessive use of drugs and alcohol or simply by running away, while still others organized themselves into unions or political movements to change the system that had led to such misery. The choices people made during the Depression, whether conscious or not, often held lifelong consequences for them.

Our questions about democracy and about individual choice turned out to be quite powerful. They were important and complex questions that did not oversimplify a crucial period in American history. They provided us with a framework to guide and focus our students' thinking as they explored the historical writings, photographs, artwork, music, and literature of the 1930s.

Finally, these were questions that are still relevant sixty years later in the 1990s. Pick up any issue of the *New York Times* and you can read about the struggle for democracy in countries all over the world. At the same time, many of our students—African American, Hispanic, Asian, immigrant, working class—face economic hardships and inequality and must, each day, make choices about the strategies they will use to survive and thrive.

Learning to Be a Learner

The second set of SPC's learning goals falls under the heading of "learning to be a learner." In this category we included essential skills and competencies necessary to become both an independent learner and an active participant in a community of learners. For the 1930s expedition we chose to concentrate on those areas we felt were appropriate for ninth graders and important in order to prepare them for serious high school work, as well as ones that would allow them to take advantage of the unique learning opportunities we hoped to provide at SPC.

We decided to concentrate on

- reading with understanding, using both fiction and nonfiction from and about the 1930s
- writing-to-learn strategies
- writing to communicate and persuade, with an emphasis on essay writing
- cooperative work group skills
- investigative skills necessary for independent research
- critical viewing

Content Goals

The third group of SPC learning goals covers subject area content. Betsey and I agreed that at the end of this expedition, we wanted students to have a clearly defined fund of knowledge about the 1930s. I have memories of my own high school history courses, most often consisting of lists to memorize—names, places, and dates, with little context offered on the teacher's part and even less interest offered on my part. Yet both Betsey and I believe that there is a foundation of knowledge worth knowing. In addition, students must be able to use their minds in a disciplined way, and that includes using their memories.

We wanted our students to be able to pass a test about the important issues, people, and events of the 1930s by the end of the expedition. We wanted them to be able to answer questions from our studies such as these: What is an economic depression? Who was Fiorello La Guardia? Can you describe a piece of New Deal legislation and the impact it had and continues to have on people's lives. What is documentary photography? What are two pieces of music you learned about during this expedition? In what ways does economic instability threaten democracy?

We also wanted our students to improve their vocabularies so that they could read and write about this period with understanding and authority.

Community and character building, learning to be a learner, and content goals—the thought and effort we put into clarifying these for ourselves before we began the expedition was time well spent. We realized that our students would have some of their own goals for this expedition, and we agreed to be vigilant and follow their leads when we noticed students' passions or curiosity come to life, but we believed it was our primary responsibility as their teachers to guarantee a rich and rigorous curriculum. Throughout the expedition Betsey and I would refer back to these goals. Every time we decided on an activity we would ask ourselves, "Does this connect to our goals?" If the answer was no, we would ask, "Why are we doing this?" and "Are we missing something that we should be doing?" These learning goals guided our work and our thinking.

Designing the Expedition

Once we had the learning goals clear in our minds, we faced the questions every teacher faces when creating a new curriculum: What do we do on Monday? What materials are we going to use? What combination of teaching and learning strategies—whole class lessons, collaborative group work, independent research—will be most effective? How much time will be spent in and out of the classroom? How will we assess what we have done?

Again, we began with a very deliberate plan for the expedition. Knowing our students, we realized that we had to find ways to make this expedition highly engaging. We decided to begin the expedition with an "immersion day" to stimulate interest in the 1930s. We knew that our students were interested in popular culture—music, games, movies, and so forth—and so we designed a day during which students looked at photos (Dorothea Lange, Walker Evans, Berenice Abbott), listened to radio show tapes (*Flash Gordon, The Shadow*), played games (Monopoly), ate food (Spam on Ritz crackers), watched movies (*Public Enemy, Radio Days*) and looked through magazines from and about the 1930s. By the end of the day we had our students' attention, if not their interest, and we were ready to begin the expedition in earnest.

For the next two weeks, we gave students an introduction to and overview of the scope of the expedition by using what Betsey called a "close and warm," "far and cool" approach. Students kept personal response logs as they read the novel *Daddy Was a Number Runner*, by Louise Merriwether, about a black girl growing up in Harlem during the 1930s, as a way of getting a "close and warm" look into the time. Simultaneously, students kept a "study guide," taking notes as we watched parts of a PBS documentary called *The Great Depression* (produced by WGBH-Boston), as a way of getting a "far and cool" look at the events and issues of the 1930s.

Following the overview, Betsey and I decided that our students would take a closer look at three aspects of the era: first, the causes and conditions of the Great Depression, including the stock market crash; second, the New Deal and its policies; and third, the trade union movement. During this time we continued to refer back to our guiding questions, asking students to examine the choices individuals made in response to the Depression and to decide how democracy was strengthened or weakened by different events that occurred during the 1930s.

We also found ourselves making constant use of the "close and warm," "far and cool" approach. We were trying to give history a human face—keeping students engaged with and connected to the curriculum through their interest in and empathy with the triumphs and defeats of real and fictional characters of the thirties. Once they were hooked, we hoped to expand their attention and push their thinking on the broader and more far-reaching ideas that the 1930s raised. It proved to be an effective strategy.

When, in *Daddy Was a Number Runner*, Francie's father could not find a job, the students' concern over the family's survival led them to look with real interest at the controversy over Franklin D. Roosevelt's New Deal policies. After reading about how Marian Anderson was prevented by the Daughters of the American Revolution from giving a concert in Washington, D.C., because she was an African American, we watched a film clip of her singing "God Bless America" in front of tens of thousands of people outside the Lincoln Memorial in a free concert, organized in part by Eleanor Roosevelt. Students were both moved and angry, and argued with each other about effective strategies to defeat discrimination then and now. After reading about how Lennie and George's dream of owning a piece of land was shattered in *Of Mice and Men*, they looked with new eyes at the devastation of the dust bowl and wondered if there could be another Great Depression in America's future.

During the next eight weeks, students read two more novels (*Of Mice and Men* and *Black Boy*), one biography of Richard Wright, and two works of nonfiction (*The New Deal*, by Gail Stewart, and a short book about the stock market crash), as well as numerous primary source newspaper articles, speeches, and diary entries.

They also did extensive writing. In "literature logs" they wrote personal responses and reflections to help them connect to and explore ideas in the novels they were reading. In "learning logs" they filled "data," "personal response," "question," and "class notes" columns while they read and discussed nonfiction texts to help them make sense of what they were reading. They wrote creative pieces—poems and dialogues based on the issues and themes we read and talked about. And they wrote more "public pieces" in which they had to communicate what they knew to a wider audience or persuade a reader of their point of view. In short, they used "writing-to-learn strategies" to help them come to personal understandings and then worked on learning to write their ideas in clear and compelling prose.

In addition, we planned weekly "team-day" trips to places in New York City connected to our expedition. We visited the New York Stock Exchange, scene of the stock market crash of 1929. We went on a walking tour of Harlem to find the YMCA where Richard Wright lived while writing *Native Son*, and we stopped at the Apollo Theater, where black celebrities have performed ever since the 1930s. We explored the Tenement Museum in the Lower East Side of Manhattan to get a picture of the living conditions of working people in the 1930s. We even found still-existing Works Progress Administration (WPA) murals in airports, post offices, and schools throughout the city. Students took notes, made sketches, and jotted down observations and questions in their team-day packets.

As the final part of their expedition and in line with our goal of helping students learn investigative skills, students took on a "biographical investigation" into the life of a historical figure from the 1930s. They set out to discover how the Depression affected the character they chose and to uncover the strategies that that person used in response to the Depression. The person they chose to investigate could be famous or infamous—politician or pilot, comedian or criminal, artist or athlete.

Students kept a "search journal" in which they documented their biographical investigations. They wrote about how they decided which person to investigate, what questions they had about the person, what problems they faced doing their research, and what they learned along the way. We required that they make use of primary source documents and, in their final report, write about what they had learned in narrative form.

Delivering the Expedition

All teachers know that nothing goes according to plan. The question is never "Will something go wrong?" but rather "What should we do when things do go wrong?" What I believe to be crucial is our ability to be flexible and creative when it comes to finding ways to support students in their efforts to achieve the learning goals for an expedition without giving up on the students, ourselves, or the learning goals. This is easier said than done.

Betsey and I gave a name to the efforts, adjustments, and strategies needed to make a plan work with a particular group of students in a particular context. We called this stage of our work "delivering the expedition." As New Yorkers we appreciate the need to deliver the goods.

From the start of this learning expedition, we faced both expected and unexpected problems. We knew that a number of our students were academically unprepared to read the novels we had chosen. As a part of our commitment to support students who are willing to cooperate but who are seriously underprepared for high school work, we did a number of things. We enlisted all our teachers and support staff to help us record each chapter of the first novel we read, *Daddy Was a Number Runner*, on separate audiotapes. Students who had difficulty keeping up with the novel could borrow the tapes. We also began offering read-aloud sessions three times a week, posting a schedule of which chapters would be read on which days. In this way, struggling readers could keep up with their classmates.

Extensive use of the PBS series *The Great Depression* provided the enrichment of primary source materials for all students as well as access to necessary information for those students who had difficulty with written text. Watching this series also gave students a chance to practice critical viewing as we explored how materials were presented from different points of view and in different media.

Although we had not originally planned to, we found ourselves making extensive use of drama techniques. In order to increase students' confidence and verbal abilities, probe complex characters and issues from different points of view, and allow all students to participate in these explorations regardless of their proficiency in reading and writing, we made use of a variety of both scripted and improvised drama activities in the classroom.

We asked students to assume the role of fictional or historical characters and to answer questions from the class about their behaviors and motivations.

This technique, called "hot seating," is used in drama classes and involves choosing a character whom students have been reading or writing about and literally putting a volunteer on a seat in the middle of the room where he or she must answer questions from the class the way the student believes the character would have answered. Students loved the drama of bringing characters to life and eagerly volunteered to be on the "hot seat."

Students improvised a "talk show" on which Louise Merriwether, author of *Daddy Was a Number Runner,* was interviewed about how and why she wrote her book. They acted out a meeting between Franklin D. Roosevelt and representatives of farm workers, labor leaders, and industrialists in which Roosevelt had to explain and answer questions about the New Deal. The most dramatic highlight of the expedition was the mock trial of George Milton for the murder of Lennie Small in the novel *Of Mice and Men.* Teams of defense and prosecution lawyers questioned and cross-examined witnesses, argued their cases for and against conviction, and made passionate closing statements in a tumultuous two-day trial. During the course of the trial, issues of mercy killing, discrimination against the handicapped, and the plight of migrant workers were raised. Ultimately, students found George guilt of homicide but recommended leniency due to extenuating circumstances.

Besides being highly engaging in and of themselves, these activities also served an important "prewriting" function as they forced students to think about their own positions on questions and issues raised in the dramatizations and prepared them to defend these positions later in writing.

Finally, we found many students unprepared, and some unwilling, to do independent research. Most students did not have library cards, and those who did were reluctant to go to the library on their own. Betsey and I set up crates of materials in the classroom which contained reference books, biographies, xeroxed photos, and articles to help launch students on their individual investigations. We also led trips to the local library and showed students how to find primary source documents.

We revised our requirement that students find at least two primary source documents for their biographical investigation, and instead asked each student to find and make a copy of the *New York Times* obituary for the person they were investigating. Now, since students were all looking for the same kind of information, we could teach them the steps to find this document and they could help each other. We did not give up on our goal of having them learn investigative skills, but we did give them a jump start and made the task more manageable.

Looking Back at the Expedition

A year later, as I look back on our Great Depression expedition, I can't help but think about what we accomplished and what we didn't. How much progress did students make toward the learning goals of the expedition? It is not an easy question to answer.

To decide how much distance you have covered, you have to know where you started. Most of the ninth graders at SPC entered the school seriously underprepared for high school work. Some had no idea of the kind of time achieving students devote to schoolwork. Others were unwilling to work hard. For those who were willing and able to put in the effort, I believe we provided the help and support they needed to make real academic progress.

Seventy-five percent of our students passed their final test on the Depression. Betsey made up a study guide to help students prepare for the test. She also allowed students to take the test a second time if they did not pass on their first attempt. A year later, those students who have remained at SPC are now tenth graders and still remember much of what they learned. Their current history teacher has told me that the students often refer to the people and events of the 1930s, connecting them to issues that the class is now studying in American history.

Since I continued to be the English teacher for SPC's upper school, I worked with the same students for almost two years. I can see for myself the progress they have made toward reaching our learning-to-be-a-learner goals. Some students came to SPC never having finished an entire book. Though not all students read all the books we worked with during the expedition, most students read most books. A few students have become avid readers. I believe that at different points in the expedition, each student experienced the power of the written word to move, challenge, and enlighten.

The students are more confident and competent writers than they were two years ago. While log entries used to be a paragraph long, students now write extensively about what they are thinking. Though they still struggle with organization and aspects of grammar and usage, most have real voice in their writing and understand the need to meet public standards when writing formal pieces so their ideas will be taken seriously by the larger world.

Some students are more willing and more skillful than others as participants in cooperative work groups, but all students have continued to work in groups—reading, writing, science study, and math survey groups. Working successfully and effectively with others is a lifetime challenge for both young people and adults. At SPC we all get lots of practice.

Students have also built on the experience of doing the biographical investigation and have completed two other assignments that required out-of-school research. Students know where their local libraries are, and most know how to find what they need there or how to ask for help.

Although I am still convinced that the ability to be a critical viewer is crucial in an age in which we receive most of our information about the world from pictures (photos, television, and movies), we were less successful with this learning goal. As much as Betsey and I promoted the idea of "video as text," when the VCR was rolled into the classroom, many students slumped down in their seats and waited to be entertained.

Most difficult to assess is the progress we made toward our community- and character-building goals. In general, I feel the question about democracy turned out to be less engaging for our students than the exploration into individual choice. It was a real stretch for students to think about the need to defend democracy when they are still too young to have participated in the democratic process and when many of them are from racial or ethnic groups that traditionally have been underrepresented in that process. I think it was the right question for our expedition, but it was abstract, and in retrospect I now see that we needed to scaffold more activities around the exploration of this complex question.

Students felt more passionate about the question of individual choice in the face of difficulty. Though there is no way to measure objectively interest and enthusiasm, questions around what people did and what they should or should not have done sparked lively discussion.

For me, the most compelling evidence for the relevance of this question is anecdotal. Six weeks into the expedition, students in one of the ninth-grade classes were having a discussion about the various strategies Richard Wright used to cope with the terrible hardships of poverty and discrimination he faced as a young man in *Black Boy*. It was clear that a few students had not read the section of the book we were talking about, and one of them began to fool around and disrupt our discussion. At that moment, another student went up to the board, pointed to the strategy "avoiding a hardship by running away," and said about the disruptive student, "That's what he's doing now, trying to escape." It was a powerful moment. A student had made an authentic connection between the curriculum and a real-life dilemma.

For me, assessment has always been a complicated issue. For a teacher, it is easy to become overwhelmed by the growing number of approaches to assessing student work—from the standards movement to calls for alternative assessment, from rubrics to test scores, from outcomes to portfolios. I sometimes worry that what gets lost in this conversation is what actually happens between young people and the adults who care about them in places called schools.

There were moments in this expedition that I will never forget: a dozen students humming "Take the A Train," by Duke Ellington, as we actually rode the A train to Harlem; fighting our way through a snowstorm to the Schomberg Library to do some research, only to find that it had been closed because of the weather, and listening to students brag about how the snow hadn't stopped us; watching five boys, whose only interest seemed to be sports, actually get excited in the library when, after a long search, the front-page obituary of Babe Ruth appeared on the microfilm screen. I do not know how to assess or count these moments, but I believe they will remain with me and my students for years to come.

7

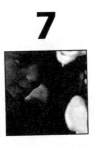

Windows into Students' Thinking:
Interweaving Curriculum and Assessment

Kathy Greeley

*In this chapter, middle school teacher Kathy Greeley discusses her grow-
ing appreciation of authentic assessment as a way of gaining insight into
students' understanding. Whether producing a play or publishing a book,
Greeley finds that children's projects provide her with concrete evidence
of their ideas; students' work becomes a "window" into their thinking.
Greeley makes a related discovery that assessment is practiced best when
it is intertwined with curriculum. Assessment is not just a final destination
in the flow of an expedition, but an opportunity for ongoing reflection.*

My own journey into the world of project-based learning and authentic
assessment began about seven years ago. It was not so much a conscious
choice to change as a necessity. Over these past several years, my seventh-
and eighth-grade classroom has become a different place. I have discovered the importance of just jumping into the unknown and experimenting,
yet this process of change has been gradual, sometimes painful, and always invigorating.

Turning Points

While I have always tried to be thoughtful about my teaching practice, I
look back to one year that, in retrospect, was a turning point for me. I was
teaching an American history class and at the time we were studying the
Constitution. I love American history (I've been an addict since the second grade), and I feel passionate about the Constitution. However, at least
so far, I had failed to inspire in my students much interest in, much less a
burning passion for, this critical document. I would try to draw them in

89

with complex, provocative questions: "Did the American Nazi Party have the right to march in Skokie, Illinois, a town with a high concentration of Holocaust survivors?" The same few hands would go up while the majority of the class sat by passively, looking rather glazed.

One day, I was determined to bring the lessons of the Bill of Rights alive. We had been looking at the Fourth Amendment, the right to be protected from unreasonable search and seizure, the day before. I secretly asked Eric, a student from the class, to be part of my plan. Eric was big and tough and never spoke up in class. At least *he* will be engaged today, I thought, even if my plan fails.

As I was talking about the colonists' being searched by British troops, another teacher (prearranged by me) knocked at the door. I put down my notes on Eric's desk, excused myself from the class, and stepped outside for about thirty seconds.

I removed my watch from my wrist and stuck it in my pocket. When I returned to the classroom, I went to pick up my notes again and stopped. "Where's my watch?" I asked Eric.

"I don't know," he shrugged, playing along.

"Look, I put my notebook and my watch right here in front of you before I stepped out of the room. Now my watch is gone. Where is it?" I could feel the tension building in the classroom. "Where is it?" I demanded.

"I don't know," Eric mumbled. "I didn't do anything with it."

"Don't give me that! I put it down here and now it's gone. And you are telling me you don't know what happened to it?" While I was intensely focused on Eric's face, I could feel twenty-five pairs of eyes on my back. "Let me see your bag."

"You can't—"

"Give it to me!" I grabbed his backpack. The class was stunned. I could feel it. They leaned forward, on the edge of their seats. *Finally* I had their attention. I was ecstatic. I started to unzip the bag. Eric, doing a great acting job, sputtered, "Y-y-you can't do that!"

"You're right!" I exclaimed. "And do you know why?" I crowed triumphantly. "Because of the Fourth Amendment to the Constitution!" On this, the tension, the attention of the class, like a balloon that has just been punctured by a pin, suddenly deflated. I had lost them again.

I left school that day feeling very frustrated. I had worked so hard to engage them, to stimulate their thinking. I didn't mind working hard, but it didn't seem right that I was doing *all* the work; the students needed to be doing some of it. I didn't know what they were thinking. I didn't know *if* they were thinking at all. How could I crack through this wall?

I spoke with a colleague about my frustration, who said, "Look, Kathy, you don't know that they are *not* thinking. Some kids just aren't all that verbal; they don't like to talk. Why don't you have them do something? Some kids like to *do*, rather than talk."

I decided to try her advice. Not being familiar or comfortable with projects or artsy stuff, I decided to have them make dioramas—those little shoebox things—relating to Constitutional issues. It was the one project-y thing I could remember having done in school myself. I asked students to bring their shoeboxes into class so I could make sure that everyone actually worked on the assignment.

I could not believe the transformation. Having something to do with their hands freed many of them to think aloud. They talked to each other about what they were doing, shared ideas, explored issues around which they would build their dioramas. They were having fun, but most were also accomplishing something. It was clear who was thinking and understanding the issues we had covered in class—and who was not. I felt as if someone had suddenly cut a window into their heads and I could get a glimpse into these students' thinking.

I began to wonder: How do I know, *really* know, what my students are thinking, what they are learning, what they know and understand? How could I find the paths into their thinking? The diorama project had taught me that I could not make assumptions about students' learning. It also showed that students needed diverse ways to share their learning. How do I let students show me what they know? Is there only one way, or are there several? How can I help them find the paths to express their thinking? My little experiment with the dioramas had opened a door. I decided I wanted to move toward doing more projects, but I was not sure how to get there.

First Steps

That summer I reconnected with an old friend, Steve Seidel, who was working with Project Zero at Harvard University. Project Zero, a research center led by Howard Gardner and David Perkins, investigates the development of learning processes in children and adults. They were particularly interested in project-based learning and authentic forms of assessment. I described my diorama experience to Steve and explained my gut feeling that I could reach more students and teach more effectively if I could go beyond talking about things and get students doing some projects. "I think we could really help each other," Steve said. "Let me know when you are ready to start."

That fall, I was teaching the Facing History and Ourselves curriculum. Facing History uses the Holocaust as a historical case study of human behavior to examine issues including intolerance, violence, prejudice, identity, and social responsibility. While studying the steps Hitler took to build a totalitarian state, we read *Animal Farm,* by George Orwell. There was a wide range of reading ability in the class. Zach and Marie understood the book as political satire, while Beth and Ketler liked reading a story about animals. However, through activities such as regular class discussions, role-plays, and character webs, every student came to enjoy the book, and all had some understanding of its parallels to the Holocaust.

When we finished the book, I thought, "Well, I guess it's time for the test." But a test seemed so flat and anticlimactic after all the work we had done on the book. Furthermore, I knew that certain students, like Beth, would not do well on a traditional pencil-and-paper test; it would not reveal what she had really learned. I could see her freezing up, deciding before she had started, "I can't do this; I don't know anything." It was important to me that she have an opportunity to show herself, as much as to show me, how far she had come in her understanding. She needed a different path. It suddenly occurred to me: "Aha! This is where I can try doing projects again." It was time to call Steve.

"Steve, I think I'm ready to try doing a project with my class, but I don't know where to start."

"What kind of projects do you want to do?" he responded.

"I don't know."

"Well, maybe you should think about *why* you want to do these projects. What do you want to know about your students' learning?" His questions pushed me to revisit my goals. What did I want my students to understand from having read *Animal Farm?* What was important to remember, to hold on to? Steve and I talked through the goals of the projects, and we talked about the nitty-gritty details. Should the projects be done singly or in groups? Should I form the groups, or allow students to choose their own partners? How much class time was I willing to give? What about deadlines?

As I look back at this time, I realize how critical it was to have support in the process of trying something new in the classroom. Most of us teach the way we were taught. When we begin to question some of the "but-that's-how-we've-always-done-its," we need support and critical feedback. I was lucky at the time to have a friend and colleague to turn to.

So we plunged in. I knew I wanted students to think about major themes from the book, such as power, stereotyping, and propaganda. But I wasn't sure about what they should actually *do*. Not being a very "hands-on" person, I turned to them for ideas. Some students chose to write a newspaper, *The Animal Farm Gazette,* focusing on the theme of propaganda. Another group did a visual art project on the theme of stereotyping and discrimination ("four legs good, two legs bad"). Others decided to do a comic book in which they explored the power theme and rewrote the ending of the book.

The room was often noisy and chaotic. At first this made me feel very uncomfortable and out of control. Sometimes I would long for the good old days of the lecture-style class. I had felt in charge then. The room had been quiet and orderly. But then I would remember that being in control had actually been an illusion. I did not know what my students were thinking; I did not know who was making sense of the lesson and who was not. The chaos was messier, but I got a lot more information.

At moments I was plagued with doubt. Is this a good use of our time? Are students really learning anything? Do the projects really demonstrate understanding? How are we building skills? But despite all this, some interesting things began to happen.

One group of seventh-grade girls decided to build a model of the farm. Melanie was a good student but very quiet. She never raised her hand in class and looked pained every time I called on her. Beth missed school a lot and carried a huge chip on her shoulder. Chavanne's main interest in school was boys. She rarely turned in homework, although she always had convincing excuses. All three girls, however, had gotten hooked on the book. Beth said, "This is the first book I ever read that I liked." They jumped into the project with enthusiasm. Melanie brought in Fisher-Price animals from home, Chavanne found a large piece of cardboard for the base, and they used other materials we had in the classroom—paint, clay, tissue paper, markers, and so forth.

They started coming in every day during recess to work on the model. They enjoyed working together and loved using their hands. I was thrilled to see these three working together and invested in the project. But as I watched the fences go up and the farmhouse get constructed, I began to wonder, What does this show about the book? They did not have to read or understand *Animal Farm* to construct a nice looking farmyard. Preschoolers do it all the time. What if a parent walked in here? "You build farmyards in the seventh grade?" What would I say? It was great to have them so engaged, but what had they learned from the book? Those seeds, or more like boulders, of doubt began to roll over me.

So I started hovering around the girls, wondering what they were thinking. "Let's put Napoleon [the chief pig] in the farmhouse to show how much he is becoming like a human." "Yeah, let's put him in bed to show how he was breaking one of the seven commandments [*No animal shall sleep in a bed*]." "And what if we have another one of the smaller pigs bringing a teacup to show how the other animals were serving him and they weren't all equal [*All animals are equal, but some are more equal than others*]." I was amazed. Throughout all our class discussions, I had never heard any of the three girls articulate their understanding of the metamorphosis of the pigs. Again, I had a window into their thinking.

About a week before the students presented the projects in class, I reported to Steve at Project Zero about our progress. I related enthusiastically the story of the girls and their farmyard. I recognized that the girls did not have the same sophisticated understanding of the political satire that the *Animal Farm Gazette* group did, but clearly they were able to demonstrate good understanding about key themes in the book. I was excited about their progress, and mine. "That's great," Steve responded. "So have you thought about how you are going to assess these projects?"

I was stopped cold. No, I had not thought about that at all. You mean, the old A, B, C grade would not work? I didn't need to ask that question. I recognized that the complexity of the students' work demanded an equally complex assessment. Just what was an "A" anyway? Did the farmyard girls deserve an A, even though I knew they lacked a sophisticated understanding of the book? What about the students who clearly understood the book, but had fooled around in class and pulled their project together at the last minute? What about the boys who had worked hard on their video project, but whose novice camera skills undermined the quality of their final presentation? What about the group that allowed one student to carry most of the load? Do they all get the same grade? The more I saw of students' thinking, the harder it was to assess, at least simply, their work.

I realized that I was looking for, and valuing, much more than just a final product. I began to spell out the different criteria: Is there clear expression of theme? Is it thoughtful and creative? Was the class presentation well organized? Did you use your time in class well? If you worked in a team, did you contribute your fair share? Did you work well with your peers? Is the final product high-quality work?

The *Animal Farm* projects took three weeks to complete. It was a time of high anxiety for me, and for the students. They were not used to making their work public. Knowing they were going to have to present their work to the class raised the stakes. But on the day of the presentation, their excitement was palpable. Beth invited her mother to come see her farm (her mother had never once come to the school in the five years Beth had been there). The principal stopped in and admired their work. The students glowed with pride.

Animal Farm marked a beginning. I had taken the first big step. I had waded into new pedagogical territory, and risked trying something different. I had made mistakes, like developing criteria for assessment at the end of the project rather than at the beginning, but the projects' successes clearly outweighed the failures. Although I did not recognize it yet, with these projects I started a process of seeing curriculum and assessment as integrally related.

"By the Way, Are We Getting Graded on This?"

The year after the *Animal Farm* projects, I launched into a curriculum that, in retrospect, could be called my first learning expedition. We were studying the Industrial Revolution, the growth of cities, immigration, and the labor movement of the late nineteenth and early twentieth centuries. As we were based in the Boston area, the resources were rich for this study. We visited the Lowell mills, we saw where the mill girls lived, we heard what power looms sound like and watched how they work. We met with an elderly man who had started working in the mills at the age of five. We studied immigration patterns in Boston, we "adopted" a family of Irish immigrants through a computer simulation program and found them housing, food, and jobs. We read the letters of early union organizers, and learned about the fight in the state legislature for the ten-hour day.

As a culminating project, we produced a play called *On the Line* that wove together the different threads of our investigations. Set in Lawrence, Massachusetts, in 1912 during the famous Bread and Roses strike, the play focuses on a young immigrant millworker's decision whether to join the strike. Having little experience in theater, we drew on parents who had theater experience and other community resources. Theater professionals, including set designers, directors, musicians, and even the playwright visited our classroom. Students plunged into designing sets, researching costumes, practicing old labor songs, and rehearsing lines. The classroom was alive. Investment in the project was high. As one student commented, "This doesn't feel like school. It feels like real work."

About two weeks before opening night, deep in the throes of production, Manoli raised his hand and asked, "By the way, are we getting graded on this?" Again, the question of assessment stunned me. I had been so wrapped up in the work of the play, I hadn't thought about individual grades. I suddenly worried that I would lose their energy and commitment to making the play if they weren't going to be graded on it. (This proved to be a groundless fear. But it raises an important question: How much do we try to motivate students with grades rather than with purposeful and meaningful work?) Being a teacher, I responded, "Of course. This *is* school." I was ready to move on, but Manoli persisted. "How?" he asked. "*How* are you going to grade us?" I was stuck. "I don't know," I said. "But we'll figure it out."

I was stumped about how to grade the students' work so I turned to the students themselves. Even though the pressures of the impending performance were bearing down, I set aside a class period to talk this issue out.

"Last week, Manoli asked if you were going to be graded on the play. I've been thinking about it, and it seems that it's an important question for us to think about. Should we grade individuals' work, and if we do, *how* do we do it? How will we know if we have done a good job?" I asked them.

"The audience will clap for us," Gloria said.

"We'll be able to see it in their faces," Sam said.

"Our friends will come up to us afterward and tell us," Leah said.

"So as a group, our audience will let us know if we were successful or not. The audience is like our test. But what about individually? Should individuals be graded?" I was puzzling over this myself. So much of our work in the play had been done as a group. How could we measure individual contributions and growth? On what would we base our evaluations? As with the *Animal Farm* projects, I was reconsidering my own goals for doing the play in the first place.

"I think so," said Xiamara. "I mean, I've worked really, really hard on this play, and I think that I should get credit for that." Other heads nodded in agreement.

"But how can you grade us?" asked Leandro. "Should somebody get a better grade just because they are a better actor?"

"Maybe someone shouldn't be graded on how good they are, but more on how hard they works at it," said Ann. "You know, if they work hard at it, they are going to end up doing their best anyway and that's what's most important."

"How do we know someone is working hard? What do we want them to be working hard at?" I asked. "What does it take to do a good job as an actor, for example?" We started to brainstorm on the blackboard.

"You've got to know your lines."

"You have to know what the lines mean, too."

"You have to speak so the audience can understand you."

"You can't crack up and 'corpse' your character."

"You should cooperate with the director."

After generating this list, I then asked students to get into committees and define criteria for evaluation in a similar way for assistant directors, set designers, musicians, publicity agents, and costume designers (every student served on at least one of these committees). Each group considered what was necessary for it to accomplish its task successfully. The assistant directors committee came up with criteria such as:

- Did you read and understand your scene before rehearsals?
- Did you make good observations and take good notes on what was working and not working in your scene?
- Did you give extra support to actors who were struggling?

The set design crew focused on other issues:

- Did you participate in the design of the set and offer creative ideas?
- Did you take initiative in solving technical problems?
- Did you help to gather materials for the set?

After each group generated its criteria, we met as a whole group again to share. After carefully reviewing each other's work, the class members agreed that we had clear and fair criteria for evaluating individual work in the play. Evaluation did not depend on natural talent or prior experience. We also realized that our list of criteria could serve as a guide for each student in preparing his or her role. For example, as an actor practiced lines at home, she could refer to the class criteria: Do I really know what my lines mean? Am I loud enough? Am I clearly enunciating each word? Did I take that suggestion from the director well? Each student could check her own progress and contribution to the whole project against common reference points.

Although at first I was frustrated with myself for not having thought about the assessment earlier, I realized I could not have generated such criteria before actually doing the work. Having never done theater, I did not know what a director did. I did not know the thinking and work that went into designing a set. I did not know how to articulate standards for acting. As we worked through these issues as a class, though, we were discovering these things together—and articulating our own learning.

When the play was over, students wrote a self-analysis based on the criteria we had created. In addition, each student responded to the following questions: What did you learn about yourself? About your class? About theater? About the life of millworkers? I read over each evaluation before writing to students with my own observations of their work. While I also attached a grade to this (I no longer feel compelled to do so), I thought that the criteria provided concrete focal points as evidence for the grade.

To me, the students' own reflections about their learning were the most powerful part of the assessment. Some who had worked very hard on the production spoke of the pride they felt in their achievement, and the reward they felt for taking risks and making a strong commitment to the process. One student who had chosen a small acting part lamented that she had not had the courage to go for a bigger role—but she would next time.

Another student surprised himself with his success on stage: "I felt like a knight in shining armor and that I could do anything!" Yet another spoke about how he did not feel totally comfortable taking part in the postproduction celebration because he knew he had not contributed as much as he could have. While the play succeeded as a group project, individuals also learned important lessons about themselves.

Road Maps to Good Work

In the afterglow of *On the Line*, I realized that the last eight weeks of school had felt different. One indicator of this change in climate had been the significantly reduced number of bathroom and water fountain requests. This is not to say that students never needed to go to the bathroom or get a drink. But when they left the room to do so, I no longer worried about keeping track of them. I didn't need to. They dashed off and were back quickly because they didn't want to miss anything. I no longer felt as if I were the engine pulling the train. We were working together. Not that it was always easy. Not that there weren't crises. Not that it wasn't exhausting at times. But the work itself had meaning to these students, and the desire to do the highest quality work was universal because the audience was real.

How could I continue to build such a climate in my classroom? I wanted to sustain that feeling all 180 days of school. Friends and colleagues told me that that was pie-in-the-sky. To have had an eight-week period of focused and inspired work from students was more than many teachers ever got. But I had had a taste and I now had a goal: to increase gradually the amount of that high-quality time each year where the work was authentic, where our audiences were real, where criteria were explicit and a useful tool, and where students held themselves to high standards.

I have not yet reached my goal, but each year I feel I get a little closer. It has been a slow yet steady process. Last year, we explored the theme of "community": What is community? When do communities work best and why? How do we build a community that respects and values the individuals within it? What are the forces that work against people's forging community? We started the year with an in-depth assessment of our own skills and gifts we brought to our school community. As part of sharing the resources of the classroom community, students researched, wrote, and illustrated picture books targeted for third graders on a subject or skill in which they had talent or expertise. In addition, each student taught a lesson about his or her expertise to our class.

I had four learning goals: (1) to introduce and practice research skills; (2) to introduce and practice the process of critiquing and revising work;

(3) to practice writing skills with a focus on clarity and developing supporting detail; and (4) to build a sense of community in the classroom by giving each student an opportunity to demonstrate a special skill, passion, or expertise.

We began the project by looking at nonfiction picture books published by professional writers. Students saw a variety of approaches to conveying information to young readers, ranging from books like *All About Whales* to *The Magic School Bus* series. While they were examining different styles of writing, they were also exposed to models of high-quality work. We wanted our picture books to look just as professional.

We invited an illustrator to class. He discussed the difference between art and illustration. He talked about how he approached assignments, what he thought about and considered before even beginning an illustration (what medium—watercolor, pen and ink, collage—best reflects the mood of the book). He taught some tricks of the trade, like working from graph paper, and brainstormed ideas with students who were unsure how to begin.

Having exposed students to the high-quality work of a professional illustrator and to published books, I encouraged them to articulate what made those models so good. "What makes a good book?" The ideas came fast: It has to capture your interest. The cover has to show what the book is about. The illustrations should communicate information in the text. One paragraph should lead to the next. The illustrations should enhance the text. The words should be easy enough for third graders to understand. The story should have a clear focus. There should be evidence of deep research, that you actually know something about your topic.

With a complex project like producing a picture book, we had to break down the different tasks and establish discrete criteria for each one. Broad or general criteria (for example, that text should be well written) did not help us improve our skills. Our criteria needed to be specific to serve as a road map for arriving at our goal of producing a high-quality product. As we looked at the growing list of criteria, we realized that they fell into distinct categories: cover design, text, and illustration.

We used this road map to guide our work. Once students had a draft of text, they met in small groups to analyze their work according to our criteria. But first I modeled this process with a draft of my own writing. Students had to refer to the criteria to analyze my text. "I like your opening paragraph." "There are too many different ideas on one page." "I'm not sure a third grader would know the word *authentic*." We also practiced giving feedback in a supportive but honest way. I wanted them to understand that how feedback is given is as important as the content of the feedback. We followed a similar protocol with drafts of illustrations and cover design.

Critique and revision became an ongoing process. Students worked on several drafts of text, illustrations, and cover design, constantly referring to the criteria for "What makes a good book?" As they assembled the books, they had to revisit the criteria yet again. Several students got frustrated and annoyed with me.

"Isn't this good enough?" Sam asked about his book, *The History of Baseball*. "I've done a zillion drafts already." While he hadn't done exactly a zillion drafts, he had done several. The book had improved significantly. The first pages drew the reader in, there was a lot of wonderful humor in it, and the illustrations were creative and carefully done. Yet the book still did not hang together. It was lacking focus, a unifying thread. We went back to the criteria: Does one page follow another? Does one paragraph clearly lead to the next?

"Your reviewers are only giving you a 3 (on a scale of 1–5) on this. Why do you think that is? Let's look more carefully at the text." On the eighth or ninth draft, the writing finally clicked in. In his end-of-the-year reflection in June, Sam wrote, "[My favorite project] I did in junior high was my picture book. I liked it so much because I worked so hard on it and in the end I had a great project. I also got the best feeling of accomplishment which you get after working very hard at something for a long time and completing it. This feeling of accomplishment is one of the greatest feelings I have ever had."

Afterthoughts

When I look back at the development of projects in my classroom, I realize just how much curriculum and assessment have become intertwined. While the dioramas and *Animal Farm* projects had been important first steps, the expert books represented the kind of integration of teaching, learning, and assessing I had been seeking. While the *Animal Farm* projects offered a window into students' thinking and gave students a variety of paths of expression, they had been done at the end of the unit as a replacement for a more traditional final test. But with the expert books, the curriculum was the project and the project was the assessment.

In the *Animal Farm* projects, criteria were developed late in the process. Using more detailed and explicit criteria gave students a clearer understanding of their grade. But, again, they were a replacement for the more traditional grade. With our expert books, criteria for excellence were developed at the *beginning* of the project. Students had clear guidelines that would inform their work. The criteria were an instructional tool. The criteria were developed *with* students by closely examining models of excellent work. By doing this, students had more ownership over the criteria and had an understanding of the high standards that were expected of them.

Designing strong projects that both engage students and enhance their skills is challenging. I had not begun my unit on *Animal Farm* with the intention of doing a project, and I had not clearly articulated my learning goals in advance. Although the projects enabled students to uncover their thinking about the various themes in the book, I lost an opportunity to develop certain skills, in writing or oral presentation, for example, through the projects. Because the learning goals for the expert projects were clearly defined before beginning the curriculum, the design was stronger and multidimensional.

About four years ago, I was asked to speak about my work with projects and assessment. To prepare for my talk, I decided that I would first outline my ideas and experiences with projects and then discuss my work around assessment. This made sense to me because it was really through my work on projects that I began to think differently about assessment ("How are we going to grade these things?"). But as I tried to plan out what I was going to say, issues of assessment kept creeping in. I then decided I had better begin my talk with assessment. But I found I could not speak concretely about assessment without grounding it in my work on projects. I went back and forth, back and forth: projects, then assessment; assessment, then projects.

And then it hit me. I could not separate them because they could not really be separated. Projects and other authentic learning tasks revealed more about students. The more I saw of them, the more I needed richer and more diverse ways of evaluating their work. More complex work demands more complex assessment.

8

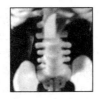

Where in the World Are We?: The Physics of Location

Donna Green, Larry Wheeler, John Sweeney, and
Deering High School students with Denis Udall

In this chapter, Deering High School (Portland, Maine) teachers Donna Green, Larry Wheeler, and John Sweeney, and their students describe an expedition that melds computer science, precalculus, and physics into a two-month study of the physics of location.

The expedition was divided into two phases. In the first, the students immersed themselves in the content of the three disciplines. During the second, they designed and carried out a major project that explored an important question or phenomenon they uncovered in the first phase.

Phase 1: *The expedition began with students learning math and physics content related to the study of location, including the principles of vectors, Kepler's laws, electricity, and magnetism. Teachers also introduced the computer program Pascal, allowing the students to design programs that would analyze and present the data they gathered from their fieldwork.*

Phase 2: *With this grounding in theory behind them, the students divided themselves into research teams based on their common interests. (Prior to the expedition, the first two weeks of school were devoted to team-building games and initiatives, in which the teachers sought to foster trust and cooperation among the students in preparation for the intensive group work during the school year. This is especially important because the composition of the research groups changes after the completion of each expedition, and thus students work closely with a large number of their classmates.) The research teams developed and wrote a research proposal that examined a question or phenomenon that grabbed the team's interest during the first phase. The teams then presented their proposals to a panel of teachers and peers who critiqued it and made suggestions for improvement. Finally, the teams carried out their research projects, which had* *to include real-world applications of theoretical material the students learned in class. The project's other requirement was that it involve computer science, mathematics, and physics. In all there were a dozen research projects going on simultaneously. Of the three projects described here, one explores robotics, another satellite dishes, and a third examines solenoids. The solenoid project is the only one of the three that does not directly involve the physics of location; however, some of the concepts were applicable.*

Students were free to move among the three classrooms during the two-hour-and-fifteen-minute block to work in small groups or to seek the assistance of a teacher. Students had a great deal of autonomy to pursue their interests and were encouraged to identify and seek out the resources they needed to complete their projects. They were also expected to conduct significant fieldwork in Portland.

At the expedition's end, the research teams developed carefully crafted exhibitions that presented their research to their classmates and the school community. The two most important components of their grade were the team's exhibition and each students' participation in designing and conducting the project.

Below are two sections. The first is a description of the projects in the students' own words. The second is devoted to comments from the teachers about the expedition as a whole. Both of these sections are based on transcribed interviews that were edited and elaborated on by Green, Wheeler, and Sweeney, and Denis Udall, the chapter's editor.

The Students' Projects

The Robotics Group

Matt McNabb, Abel Russ, Shiva Gupta, and Alex Ruthenburg

We knew we had to stick to the topic of vectors. At first we just wanted to prove a few theorems, but one member of our group suggested building a robot arm. A robot arm changes degrees and angles in three-dimensional space, so we knew it involved vectors and would be an interesting thing to look at.

We quickly realized that the project was too large for us. We visited Nichols of Portland where they use robots in the manufacturing process. The technician there did not know much about matrix transformation,[1]

---

[1] In this section the students refer to two related terms: multiple coordinate systems and matrix transformations. When a physicist wants to describe precisely the configuration of something in space, she or he first chooses a coordinate system with which to describe it. Basically, a coordinate system is a way of labeling all the points in space that are possible for the object you are describing to occupy. Imagine you want to describe the location of a billiard ball on a table. A coordinate system would be similar to a set of points along one

because he used a computer programmed already to perform the functions. But he did know a thing or two about aligning robots to perform specific tasks. He broke the news to us: it would take months of work and would cost a lot of money to build a robot arm. He also made us realize that building one involved a lot of things we knew very little about, like gear ratios and electronics. Instead, our teachers suggested that we locate a preassembled robot arm and delve into transformation matrices. Transformation matrices enable us to move an arm from one point in space to another. (Actually, we found out later that it would have been possible to build part of an arm, but we would not have gotten into matrix transformation or the interface chip with the computer, and so it wouldn't have been as interesting.)

Robot arms consist of a number of different joints or axes. Ours has five: the base, shoulder, elbow, wrist, and hand. The computer can move only one axis at a time. Our task was to find where the arm was in space and then locate another point where we wanted to move it to. Then we had to move each axis to get it there. The computer program (and the math involved) helped us tell each axis how far to rotate. It finds exactly where the arm is in three-dimensional space and moves it to the new coordinate.

The computer program can tell where the arm is through the Hall Effect sensors we've mounted on it. There are five of them, one for each joint. We've attached them to the body of the arm, and their wires run directly to the computer. First, we decide where we want the joint to stop, and then we attach a sensor at that point. Next, we attach a magnet to the joint so when it moves, the magnet lines up with the sensor, and this signals the computer to stop the joint exactly at that spot.

Our first task was to program the arm to pick up a roll of tape, move to a different location, drop it into a container, and return to its original position. What we're trying to do now is employ matrix transformations so that the arm will go right to any location and we won't have to spend an hour preprogramming each rotation. We've pretty much figured out the math, but the next step is making it actually work.

---

wall, to specify its horizontal position, along with a set of points along a wall at a right angle to the first one, to specify its vertical position. In three dimensions you would need to add another coordinate axis to have a complete coordinate system. A matrix transformation, in this context, is a way of shifting from one coordinate system's description of an object to another, alternative coordinate system's description of that same thing. Suppose you are using one coordinate system to describe the position of a baseball in the air. Then suppose you decide that another coordinate system is more convenient. Using the mathematical operation of a matrix transformation you can *transform* from one coordinate system to another, from one description of the baseball to another.

That's the physics of it, but there were a lot of quirks along the way. For example, the computer's transformer, which operates the special robotics chip we installed, got so hot that it shut down. We found out just how hot when we burned ourselves touching it! So we had to hook up a tiny fan to cool it enough to keep it running. Another problem we faced was that the rotations of the arm are measured in time instead of degrees. Much to our surprise, we couldn't use a polar coordinate system to figure out how many degrees each part of the arm should move. In comparison, it's fairly difficult to measure time—one second is about thirty degrees, two seconds is eighty degrees, and so on. This has been much more complicated than we thought it would be. So this project was full of innovative solutions like that. This is the stuff you just don't find in the books on this subject.

The way our group functions is that we divvy up the tasks, and then we all go off and work on our own. Later we come back together and explain our work to each other. It's better this way, because while you're working it's hard to explain it to someone else. It slows you down incredibly. Had we all worked together on every aspect of the project we wouldn't have gotten the same amount of work done. It's a good way of managing our time. And at the end of the week we do, out of necessity, meet to discuss what we've done. We don't really feel that we're missing out by not knowing exactly what each of the others is doing. We'll miss out in terms of the actual conceptualization, but at the end each of us will be able to grasp the whole.

This class has been different from others. The one question every student asks his or her teacher is, "Why do I need to learn this? What possible application could this have in the real world?" Invariably the teacher doesn't have a good answer. We remember doing matrices a couple of years ago, and we asked the teacher if there were any applications, and he couldn't think of one. Another thing this class does is help us to explain and organize our ideas so we can present them to others. We have to convince our audience that we know what we're talking about. Along the way, we've learned how to craft a really nice presentation.

The Satellite Dish Group

Hannah Flynn, Zack Keefe, Sarah Palmer, and Sara McIlveen

[From the team's research proposal] *Our goal is to teach ourselves about the uses of satellites and their technology in order to operate a satellite. We are hoping that through our research we will be able to discover how satellite dishes are aimed in order to receive transmission from satellites that are sending information.*

At first we were at a total loss. We didn't know where to begin our project. We had learned about vectors, waves, and focal points through books, but we had no idea about their applications in the world. For instance, we never knew how to use direction-cosine;[2] we just knew that it involved an equation, but we never knew what it was used for. So we talked to Mr. Sweeney, and he sparked our interest by asking us about things that you can't see, like satellites. He asked us, "How do you know where they are? And how do you point them so they hit something here on earth?" This really engaged us because we had learned the math, but here was a chance to go outside the school to see how people really use this stuff. In math courses students always ask their teachers, "When am I going to need this?" And now we had an opportunity to find out.

We began with the question "How do they know how to point satellite dishes so that they receive satellite transmissions?" First we did the math, and we discovered that it was possible to answer our basic question through direction-cosine. But for the longest time we had no idea if that's the way it's actually done. We knew we could figure it out on paper by establishing three separate axes in three-dimensional space and then finding the angle at which to point it from each of the three axes. But here we were in the middle of our project, still trying to find out how they actually do it in the real world. That was kind of scary! We worried that the right answer might have nothing to do with what our project was supposed to be about.

People who have dishes in their backyards told us that the cable company just sets them up with no regard to how they're pointed. No one we spoke with thought that when Mr. Cableman comes to install your dish he takes out a protractor and does a few calculations there in your backyard. That seemed pretty unlikely.

We located a technician at the local cable station who told us how they aim the dishes, and it turned out to be almost exactly the way we did it. So we were right after all. He actually took out his instruments right there and showed us how it's done. And because we had already done a lot of research about satellites we could digest what he was talking about. He told us, "You measure this line here and this line here." And we said, "Hey, that's vector dishing!" or "Hey, that's a focal point!" And it really brought it home. Those were concepts we had learned in class but didn't really understand until that moment.

We spent a lot of time researching in the library, but we learned more in that hour and a half with the cable technician than at any other time. Prior to the field trip we had been aimlessly researching things, and of

---

[2] Direction-cosine is an alternative form of coordinate system, the purpose of which is to specify the position of an object in space.

course we had our theorem, but we didn't know if it was right. But once we knew that our original idea was correct we were much more directed.

Finally, we took all the information we had gathered and made a model. Mr. Sweeney suggested using a laser to simulate a satellite transmission, and he helped us with the problem of focal point. We remembered that we had learned about focus in an earlier class, but for the life of us we just didn't get it. It really bugged us because we like to understand something completely. The project really brought together a lot of things we've learned throughout the semester, such as focal points, and it allowed us to see how they're interconnected.

When it came time to begin thinking about the presentation, we had so much information we were kind of overwhelmed. We didn't know what to use and where to put it all. A lot of the problem was order; for us to explain one idea we'd also have to explain three other concepts as well. There was also another problem: how do we take what we learned in two weeks and cram it into a twenty-minute presentation? So we decided to lay a foundation early in the presentation so that we could get into the more complex stuff later on. The presentation definitely helped us to organize what we had learned.

The Solenoid Group

Ben Herrick, Jon Doughty, and Justin Anderson

[From the team's research proposal] *Our goal is (1) to illustrate in a real physical context the mathematical concepts of vectors and vector cross products; (2) to create a working solenoid utilizing concepts from mathematics and physics; and (3) to verify that a cross product of two vectors can be mathematically illustrated using our solenoid.*

At first we thought that the way a solenoid works is that whatever is inside gets magnetized really powerfully and this propels it out like a gun.[3] We also knew it was somehow an illustration of the cross product. So we presented our proposal to the class and said, "This is the best we can do right now, given what we understand."

---

[3] Simply put, **solenoids** are electrical-mechanical motors. They are usually used as mechanical switches, to push or pull on things in a car engine, for instance, or an electrical device. Thus, the students' homemade solenoid, with the wires coiled around it, is basically an electromagnet. When a current runs through the wire, a magnetic field (sometimes called "**magnetic flux density**") is created inside the tube. The magnetic field inside the tube runs parallel to the tube's inside. The more wraps of wire there are per inch or the stronger the current through the wire, the stronger the magnetic field inside will be. The students' solenoid had a small wooden stick that extended into the tube and sat on a

Once we got started, Mr. Sweeney showed us a solenoid, and we noticed that there was this board inside with a wire running around the end of it. After messing around with it for a while we realized that the board wouldn't balance, and we were kind of puzzled about that, because we knew there was a cross product—two intersecting forces on a plane and another force perpendicular to the plane. So we kept looking at it, and we finally figured that flux density was the magnetic field. And at one point Mr. Sweeney said, "The current is the vector you're going to cross." This led us to believe that the cross product had to be the current across the end of the board because that was the only thing we had that was perpendicular to the other two vectors. But we still had to figure out which way the force went. We asked him, "What do you mean by 'crossing'? We don't understand how and where it's crossing." And he said, "What's crossing is the current through the wire on the board." But we still didn't know if it was the current across the end, or the current through the entire wire wrapped around the board. We had to figure that out for ourselves.

Next, we got to the point where we realized that the board inside the solenoid would pull down because of the way the cross product works. Then, rather suddenly, we found that we could measure the strength of the force by putting small weights on the opposite side of the board from where the current was running. We shared this idea with Mr. Sweeney, and sure enough he told us that's exactly how it works. Later he showed us how to fine-tune our experiment.

We also did a fair amount of reading. One of us started reading about magnetism, another about solenoids. We found out that when a wire is moved in a magnetic field a current is created, and if a wire has a current running through a magnetic field it will move. So we began to get a better understanding that a magnetic current is created perpendicular to the wire. The teachers provided guidance when we got stuck, but we also learned a lot from messing around with the solenoid. We'd hook things up or stick something inside, like a nail. Sometimes the solenoid would create a mag-

---

fulcrum inside, so that it rocked like a seesaw. A wire was fed in and followed a path that took it across the inside end of the stick, and then back out. When the students applied an electrical current to the wires on the outside of the tube they created a magnetic field inside it. The magnetic field caused the wire on the stick to feel a force whenever a current ran through it. The direction and magnitude of the force was calculated by taking the "cross product" of the magnetic field and the forces of the electrical current (or "vectors"). In the case of the students' solenoid this force pushed down the end of the wooden seesaw inside the solenoid. The students measured the force by placing small weights on the other end of the board. The stronger the magnetic force acting on the end of the board inside the solenoid, the more weights they had to put on the end of the board outside to balance it.

netic field strong enough to pull the nail. Other times it wouldn't pull the nail at all.

At one point we talked to a Deering teacher who used to be an electrical engineer, and he told us about flux density. And then we had to go find out what that is. This was a key concept, because if we hadn't known what flux density was, then we couldn't have gotten as far. But our teachers never said, "This is flux density, and this is how it applies to your problem." Instead, what they said was, "You're looking at flux density, go look it up." So we looked it up and found out the definition of the word. And when we needed to understand it in greater detail, Mr. Sweeney would define it a bit more and we'd apply it a bit more. But his help always fit with where our understanding was at the moment—it took us just that little bit further.

We had also read some stuff on magnetic laws and positively and negatively charged particles. And that's when we discovered a theory about electromagnetism that we thought would enable us to build a solenoid. The theory didn't make a lot of sense to us, but we still thought it would be an interesting thing to pursue.

We built a large solenoid, thinking that the bigger it was the more force it would have. But we found it to be extremely weak. We ran the wire through the amp meter and discovered there was so much resistance that every time we increased the current to where we could feel a magnetic pull, the meter would shut down because you have to run a lot of current through it for it to remain on. There wasn't even enough force to pull a nail. We were always comparing our home-built solenoid to the preassembled one Mr. Sweeney supplied us with. Mr. Sweeney's had enough current to pull nails.

Finally, we came upon a formula for measuring flux density as a ratio of the number of coils of wire in a length of solenoid. That made a lot of sense because if a wire creates a magnetic field around itself, then the more coils you can squish in a small space, and the more powerful the magnetic field will be. Sure enough, we compared the two solenoids, and we saw there were more coils in the preassembled one than in our home-built model.

So we drew a lot from the teachers. We were always asking, "Can you show us this?" or "Can you tell us this?" But the questions came from us. Like, "It's not working the way we thought it would; why? What do we need to do differently? How do we need to change our thinking?" And they would say, "Why don't you set up your solenoid and see what happens?"

So this project was like doing a jigsaw puzzle. But it wasn't like doing it from the edges in. It was more like coming up with the pieces; some of it we filled in ourselves and sometimes we had to say, "We're looking for a piece about this big." And Mr. Sweeney would say, "Look, it has an edge about like this and another like this."

The Teachers' Reflections

Donna Green, Larry Wheeler, and John Sweeney

We helped them only in the sense that they would sit down and tell us their story and we wouldn't let any poor physics go by.

We were fairly certain that the solenoid team was going in a direction that wouldn't be productive, but we let them go. It cost them time, but in the long run they got to know the territory better. As a scientist, you're always taking paths that dead end. The important thing is for these young people to see when they're at a dead end and know what to do when they recognize it.

We helped them only in the sense that they would sit down with us and tell us their story and we wouldn't let any poor physics go by. So if they started using terms incorrectly we'd stop them. We'd never say, "You ought to quit this and go this way." Instead, we'd ask a question, for instance, "Is there any way you can control the strength of this magnetic field with your apparatus?" We felt that if they tackled questions like that they'd come up with their own answers.

With regard to the satellite team, we suggested the project idea, but they went further than we anticipated. Locating the planets and satellites is a focus of the expedition, so they were familiar with geosynchronous satellites. They came to us for help in choosing a project, and we asked them, "How do you locate where a satellite is?" And they made the connection: "Hey, we've looked at those things [satellite dishes], and they don't move around. When you set them up they're pointing at the same spot all the time." They made the connection that there must be a geosynchronous satellite involved, and they took it from there.

You have to give different groups different amounts of structure.

The solenoid team developed their own project. They started by asking us, "What do you have in the way of equipment?" And we put everything out on the table. On the other hand, it was a great comfort for the satellite team to have a well-defined project with clear parameters, whereas the solenoid team was less particular about where they were going to end up. The satellite team knew they were entering charted terrain, so there was a safety net of sorts. The solenoid team didn't want a net.

A large part of the difference between these two teams was that the students in the satellite group were used to having content fed to them. But we've all seen tremendous growth in them as a result of this project—they're much more self-starting now. They have a lot more confidence and a kind of take-charge attitude—if they have a question, they'll ask, and if they need to make an appointment outside the school, they'll do it.

Fortunately, we didn't really have to deal with the problem of some teams finishing their projects before others. It's true that some groups need more time than others. But if the projects are sufficiently complex and rich—if they're pitched at high level—then the students will never really reach the bottom within the time frame we give them.

There's an interesting question: Why are some students more willing than others to take risks? From the physics point of view, being able to look at the data and make decisions about what's essential to answering a problem and what's peripheral is a skill we'd like all of them to develop, but it involves a level of inquiry that a lot of young people are uncomfortable with. In their education they've grown accustomed to the idea that you're not supposed to make mistakes. Everything has to work the first time around. It's tough to convince them that that's not really where the learning takes place.

There's a tendency for students to gravitate to their strengths.

Each individual has a strength that he or she brings to the group. Sometimes we've seen individuals pursue their interests in ways that undermine the collaborative nature of the projects. We try to engineer away from it, but we see it happening. It's a kind of balancing act. Not everyone has to be present while each member is doing his or her work. But we have to be careful to structure time for the team members to share with each other what they've learned.

For instance, a young man in the solenoid group went just about as far as he could with the Pascal program he wrote for doing the solenoid computations. But he did that at the expense of his understanding of the physics. It was the job of another of his teammates to go off and develop the physics component. Each might not be as well versed as the other in his or her respective fields, but for us as teachers, what's important is that we make sure students are learning how to think, how to dig, and how to read. Then over the long haul they're probably learning more than if we tried to force all of them to do exactly the same thing.

The whole point of interdisciplinary work is exploring the places where these fields overlap.

Unfortunately, teachers often reduce the complexity of a subject before handing it to students; they round off the rough edges. But if we respect the natural complexity of the subject matter, students are more likely to see connections between disciplines; the boundaries between subjects begin to blur. Students begin by studying one phenomenon and end up following their leads into other areas. We like that they're going in all these different directions because the whole point of interdisciplinary work is that you can explore the places where fields overlap. Each is not contained in its own box.

For example, at the outset the solenoid group didn't really have any idea about voltage or magnetism. The current expedition is about location, and so we haven't really covered magnetism and electricity in class in the depth they needed to pursue their project. They really knew very little about these subjects when they started. But they have learned a remarkable amount on their own. They had to in order to get to the bottom of their questions about solenoids. When they began studying magnetism they brought in a compass and discovered that the magnetic field of a solenoid is stronger than the field of the earth. So they started off with magnetism, but eventually found their way back to the location theme.

The depth of this expedition far outweighs the content we haven't covered.

We went through a period when we worried about the content. At the end of the year they still have to do well on national achievement tests. The content for this course is not what we would normally have covered in a physics or math class. But we have done so much else with these students as far as the product, the process, the problem solving, and the team work. We feel that this expedition far outweighs what we haven't covered in the content. If we went through the standard topics in the traditional way there would be very few young people at the end of the year who could do anything meaningful with what they had learned.

The main difference between these students and those in other, more conventional classes we've taught is that these are what we call brave learners. They're not afraid to step into a situation they're unfamiliar with. Also, in other classes students rarely seem to care much about problems like vector cross product. It's just another thing they had to learn. Few would really understand it because we didn't spend enough time on it. With this group, they took it apart and put it back together in so many ways that they seem to understand it far better than any group we've worked with before.

We were also concerned about getting enough content across so they could do something. It's always a problem starting out. There's a basic vocabulary. There are some ground rules in each of the disciplines. We were faced with this at the beginning of the year. How do we get them started on the theme? So, again, it's a bit of a balancing act. In the end, they will want to do well on the achievement tests. And yes, we do have to give them enough content in the beginning to make the expeditions meaningful. One way we found around this dilemma is to spend the last several weeks of the course preparing for the tests. It's a bit of a trade–off. We believe this expeditionary methodology is how one really learns, but we also know we live in the real world.

There's no other way to work collaboratively than to be honest about each other's gaps.

When we started out, we used to try to get a perfect fit between the physics and math components, but we discovered it was very difficult to do. Instead, what has worked very well is the idea of a theme that is broad enough to fold everything into it, a kind of big conceptual umbrella.

We're unique in that all three of us know something about each other's fields. I can walk up to John and ask him about a physics problem that I don't understand, and he knows he can do the same with me when it comes to computer programming. There's a lot of trust that goes into it. But there's no other way to work collaboratively than to be honest about each other's gaps. So there are two important aspects to this collaboration. First, there has to be trust. And second, we have to have a pretty solid understanding of each other's fields. We're asking these young people to be interdisciplinary. It would be hard if we didn't know much about each other's disciplines. How could we possibly model interdisciplinary learning if we didn't practice it ourselves?

For the next time.

There are at least four key things we discovered along the way that we should make sure to include next year. First, there should be a clearly defined theme that drives the expedition. Second, it's extremely important that the students be brought into the process aspect of the class—that is, the group nature of all the work, especially for the research projects. But once they are, you've got to give adequate value to it. You have to build it into the grade structure. Third, as teachers we have to be patient and allow sufficient time for the expeditions to play themselves out. We need to make certain not to rush things even when we find ourselves wanting to move faster. Finally, we saw that the students were capable of working maturely and independently outside the school environment. We need to remember that when the conditions are right they are perfectly able to direct their own learning outside of the school grounds.

9

Water: A Whole School Expedition

Ron Berger

In this chapter Ron Berger describes a yearlong interdisciplinary expedition on the theme of water which involves his entire elementary school and the surrounding community. Students from kindergarten through sixth grade study water as a resource, along with its physical properties and biology. The aesthetic dimensions of water—its presence in literature, music, song, poetry, and painting—provide a common thread that runs through the students' investigations. Children draw upon the talents and interests of town residents, local experts, and a college professor and his class to help them with their research. As a culminating study, students tested the town's drinking water for lead and sodium contamination. The students keep the community and the local paper apprised of their findings. But as the testing progresses, Berger and his colleagues begin wondering if they have a public health crisis on their hands.

In my school, curriculum and instruction are centered in thematic studies. Teachers design original units to use with their classrooms, and these units represent long-term expeditions into different worlds of knowledge. Every once in a while the staff feels brave enough, or crazy enough, to attempt a whole school expedition. The most vast and ambitious of these was a yearlong whole school journey into the theme of water. For an entire year, kindergarten through sixth-grade students were immersed, so to speak, in literary, artistic, mathematical, ecological, political, athletic, scientific, and playful aspects of this broad topic.

My fear in trying to recreate this study to share with others was that my fondness for metaphor and my terrible sense of humor would join forces against my will to insert puns into every sentence. I found myself describing students as "plunging into studies" or "getting their feet wet" with activities. I myself have been "wading" through data in preparing this account, "filtering out" the important issues. In describing the most intense moments of this study, when it sank in that the research of students could uncover serious health hazards for town citizens, creating a panic for families, I remembered how often we felt that we were "over our heads" in taking on this project. I've tried valiantly to cleanse my language of this affliction. Kidding aside, this process made clear to me the ubiquitous and almost archetypal presence of water images in our language and in our thinking.

While it's important to explain the study's goals, activities, scope, and sequence, I also want to convey some of its spirit and life. A goal such as "investigation of aquatic reptiles" is less vivid than my memory of two sixth-grade girls stalking a large water snake through a weedy swamp, waist-deep in muck and water, then hitting an unexpected underwater hole and disappearing below the surface of the water.

I think of first graders, digging channels in the sand, struggling with giant buckets of water to begin the life of a stream. I think of third- and fourth-grade students on a rowboat out in the middle of a town lake, carefully lowering into the water a clever homemade water-sampling contraption built of rope, hardware, duct tape, cork, rocks, a wine jug, and a thermometer. More than anything, I think of the excitement and fear in the classroom as my students compiled and reported data from town well samples. The children, teachers, town families, the town board of health, and the local newspapers were awaiting these results with impatience and apprehension. But everything was in the children's hands, and there was no rushing them. With the lives and health of real people at stake, the students refused to post anything until it had been checked and rechecked. They were as terrified of making a mistake as we were of uncovering a crisis. This was serious business!

Let me put this study in context. I teach sixth grade in a rural public school in western Massachusetts. It's a small school in the woods, financially poor but rich with ideas and energy. At the time of this study we had about 140 students and seven teachers. We are privileged in having a small, creative staff who respect and enjoy each other. We are anything but privileged in the physical and financial conditions of our work.

Every few years we muster up the courage to organize a theme of study for the entire school. As with many phenomena in life (childbirth is an example used by some mothers), after a few years we seem to remember the good parts of these whole school extravaganzas and forget the degree of pain, problems, and mess. Even though every teacher on our staff has individual talent and dedication in developing his or her own classroom themes, schoolwide themes require more time and a much higher degree of coordination. With time, though, the memories of headaches fade and the staff (at least the more optimistic or senile among us) grows nostalgic for that wonderful celebration of learning, discovery, and sharing that permeates the school during such an adventure.

The impetus for choosing water as our topic of study was an interesting one. One of our staff, third- and fourth-grade teacher Ken Lindsay, took a year's leave of absence from school to pursue a number of educational projects. During this year, the town where he lived became embroiled in a frightening water contamination crisis: private wells had become contaminated with dangerous pesticides from agricultural sources. Ken jumped into a leadership role in the citizens' group investigating this crisis, fighting for well testing and emergency water distribution. (Several years later these efforts finally paid off. The town agreed to build a $4 million water system, partially funded by the state, to replace half its delivery system for private wells.) Needless to say, Ken got little else done that year. Ken returned to school the next year with a new expertise and sensitivity concerning water as a resource for life. The rest of the staff, having had our own wells tested during that panic year, had been awakened also. We felt a responsibility to impress upon children the importance of this issue. And so, when discussions began in January about a possible topic for our school study next year, water rose quickly to the top of the list.

Planning

The staff began that February and March with brainstorming sessions of all the possible topics, activities, and concepts that could fall under the umbrella of water studies. And, as with my problem with wet metaphors, we found the topics to be almost endless. Our first session yielded about one hundred ideas and resources. From here, the planning began. I was lucky enough to work with Ken on the smaller staff committee entrusted with shaping this vast list into something manageable.

Ken and I wrote a small grant proposal, seeking state funds, and were lucky enough to receive a $3,000 grant for staff development around this theme. This money had a great impact on our planning, as it allowed us to hire experts to teach the staff, and fund educational activities for staff members.

The greatest resource a school has when it embarks on a learning expedition is the creativity, energy, and cooperative spirit of the staff. This is a resource, like water, that is often taken for granted: it is drawn upon constantly, with little effort to renew and refresh it. Our project committee worked with the staff to design a spectrum of staff activities to address this. These activities included trips: a boat trip down the Connecticut River with an expert guide, a canoe trip for staff and families, and even a whale watch off the coast of Massachusetts.

These activities were intended to accomplish three things: first, to inspire the staff—to build interest, enjoyment, cooperation, and spirit in a watery world; second, to provide diverse forums for staff to plan and work together in small groups or as a whole group, free from school pressures; and third, to provide training experiences for the staff in different scientific and ecological aspects of water so that we would have a base of knowledge for beginning.

Whenever possible, we included the full school staff, not just the teachers; the cafeteria manager, secretary, custodian, and all support staff were invited to our boat trips, whale watch, and lake studies. In practice, the activities did not always focus on a single goal, such as morale, science education, or planning time. Many events addressed all these goals at once.

We also arranged for a series of workshops for staff members during the year on a host of topics. Three local educator/experts presented scientific workshops on acids/bases and pH experiments in the classroom, the biology of pond life, and soap bubbles as a curricular study. A parent who was an expert in the life cycles of fish presented information, and three experts in water resources (one, our own Ken Lindsay) gave presentations on watersheds, wells, and water, and septic systems. Some of these workshops and presentations were repeated for children as a large group or in classrooms, but it's significant that they were first done for the whole staff without students present, providing time for questions and brainstorming of applications without the distraction of simultaneously managing students.

The Study Begins

We loosely divided the water study into three phases. The fall would focus largely on water as a resource, the winter would focus on the physical properties of water, and the spring on the biology of bodies of water. It was difficult to keep to these distinctions once we got going (when you've got three children out in a rowboat, it's hard to tell them to ignore the fish and think only about water temperature). The phases were helpful in organizing the major emphasis of our investigations in the classrooms and the school. The aesthetic aspects of water—watercolor painting, the literature of water and the sea, water poetry and stories, whaling ballads and water songs, sand castles, and so forth—were a thread that ran through all phases in myriad ways.

We wanted teachers to have the flexibility and support to pursue their own water units and projects within the classroom. It was vital to us, though, that the knowledge gained in these classroom studies contribute to our whole school understanding of water. We planned regular assemblies where students from all classes, from kindergarten to sixth grade, could share their learning as "teachers" for the school. Our school library was the site of these assemblies, and maps and exhibits were exhibited there as our work grew. Many of these assemblies were run by students themselves, with much coaching, rehearsal, and preparation of diagrams and illustrations to ensure clear lessons. During the most heated points of the study, these assemblies occurred every week or two.

Field trips and visits by local experts have always been key to our classroom thematic studies. Not only do they connect the children to the real-life aspects of their work, but they inspire the students to look at resources—whether museums, libraries, people, or ponds—with the respect and excitement that come to newly emerging experts. We generally bring the students on trips or invite experts into the classroom after students have gained a foundation of knowledge and investment in the topic. As the culmination of a study, these events can be wonderful, as students already have the deep background and interest to be polite, absorbed, and excited guests or hosts. Because they are striving to become experts themselves, they often treat expert guests with a hero's welcome.

We used a variety of trips and presentations with children, with single classes, pairs of classes, or the whole school. We visited the New England Aquarium, local fish hatcheries, a fish ladder for salmon and shad on the Connecticut River, a whale watch in Gloucester, Massachusetts, and college laboratories, and took countless trips to local lakes, ponds, streams, bogs, and swamps. The guest experts spanned a wide range, from geologists to parents who worked in fisheries to a folk singer who taught us water songs.

We have a small lake in our town, Lake Wyola, which became a center for our studies. In bathing suits or boots, with field nets, ropes, clipboards, buckets, bottles, bags, and thermometers, students ventured around, in, and on top of the lake. Some of this was done by individual classes. The third and fourth graders went door to door around the lake with a survey for lake dwellers on how they used the lake. They also measured water temperature and acidity in the lake from the shore and from boats, looking for stratified layers and patterns of water movement, and also examined its surrounding streams and swamps. They monitored pH as an indicator of the lake's health for sustaining wildlife. The fifth grade studied fish populations through observation of nests and by using giant seining nets to collect specimens. The sixth grade studied the glacial formation of the lake and its geology, prepared a depth map of the lake through the use of a motorboat with a sonar "fish finder" instrument, and collected and studied reptiles, amphibians, insects, and all sorts of large and small invertebrates.

In addition to these classroom studies, there were two whole school "Wyola Days," one in September and one in June. Everyone—children, teachers, custodian, cook, parents, and principal—got wet on these days. On Wyola Days, students from the kindergarten, first- and second-grade classes joined in with their own projects—sailing homemade yachts, studying river and stream movement, building sand castles, and painting scenes— while the third through sixth graders continued their various water studies. The students also delved into local history and lore. Two older town residents, "the keeper of the dam" (an official town post, which pays five dollars a year) and the owner of "the pay beach" and campground, met with students and teachers to give some background on the lake over the years. These Shutesbury elders were kind enough to repeat their reminiscences and lessons to different groups of students throughout the day. On this day, the staff learned as much as the children.

We included physical science studies of water from many sources; the most significant were units prepared by the wonderful *Elementary School Science* program. We used unit guides, which were often accompanied by kits that we could purchase or borrow, at many grade levels. All contained hands-on experimental work and lessons in recording and interpreting data. The lower grades used units in *Sink or Float* and *Clay Boats;* the middle grades, *Color Solutions*; and the upper grades, *Kitchen Physics* and *Stream Tables.* A workshop by a local educator/naturalist prepared all teachers to investigate the physics of soap bubbles with their classes, and a workshop by a science teacher equipped the upper-grade teachers to investigate acids and bases with their classes through preparing a homemade litmus indicator, a solution of red cabbage juice.

Biological studies of whales, fish, aquatic reptiles, amphibians, and invertebrates occurred at different levels. These classroom units ranged from a few weeks in length to a few months. A local educator/naturalist not only taught staff and children techniques to collect and identify pond and stream life, but also loaned the school equipment to do so, including a projection microscope that turned barely visible specks in pond water into monsterlike creatures on the classroom wall. Classrooms were overflowing with aquatic life; we purchased ten-gallon aquariums in great number, as well as buckets and plastic trays. Fish eggs, frog eggs, salamanders, insect larvae, diving beetles, perch, and small-mouth bass consumed our days. The bubbling sound of air pumps was a constant drone. That spring the school was filled with paintings, drawings, models, poems, and stories of whales, fish, and dragonflies (in my classroom, even water fleas and leeches).

We searched for literature that embraced watery topics, from sailors and the sea to rivers, rain, snow, ice, fish, whales, and turtles. Teachers and students read books aloud at all levels—from *Swimmy* , by Leo Lionni, to *Huckleberry Finn*, by Mark Twain. Some books were used in reading group studies. In addition to our classroom work, our art specialist and music specialist wove watery themes into their work with classes, and our spring school concert was a celebration of water.

Much of the water project work was interdisciplinary, to the extent that it would be impossible to categorize as science, art, math, or language studies; it was all at once. When first- and second-grade students studied fish, they had live fish on every table in the classroom. Children counted them, observed their habits, drew pictures of them, kept journals of their life cycles, created safe experiments for them, and wrote poems and stories about them. These students read fictional and nonfictional stories about fish. Fish words became their vocabulary and spelling challenges. They did watercolor paintings of fish, tempera paintings of fish, tissue paper collages of fish, collages of crayon and ink-stamped fish, and stuffed fish models. They observed fish in the classroom, fish in hatcheries, fish at an aquarium, and fish in local ponds and streams. Students probably couldn't have told you what was science and what was art, but they could have told you an awful lot about fish.

Fit to Drink

We began the year with a focus on water as a resource. Though drinking water may seem like a less compelling subject for children than water snakes or whales, it emerged as the most powerful and passionately pursued topic of the year. Few citizens, child or adult, appreciate the precious resource of clean drinking water that we enjoy in this country. Only in severe water shortages or contamination crises do we begin to see what we usually take for granted. As a staff, we felt it was important to foster an ecological consciousness in our students about water protection and conservation—not through lectures but through real work.

For an adult, raw statistics themselves can be jolting. The average American directly uses about 160 gallons of water per day and indirectly uses about 1,800 gallons, compared with an average of 12 gallons per day for persons in less developed nations. While about 40 percent of the world is without clean, safe drinking water, we use about 60 gallons of clean water to wash a load of our clothes, and about 25,000 gallons of clean water to produce one pound of beef for human consumption.

These kinds of statistics are not always real for children. We needed other strategies to introduce them to the notion of water conservation and protection. A first-grade teacher had each child keep a water log. In school and at home, students kept track of how many times water was used, for drinking, cleaning, flushing toilets, watering the lawn, or for any other purpose. They got parental help when needed, and parents were encouraged to join the study. For a limited time, this teacher allowed students to use water only with a "water ticket," so that they could experience what the world would be like with water rationing. Students learned how much water can be wasted from a leaky faucet by doing experiments with slow drips from the classroom sink. Even if the figure of 200 million gallons, which is the estimated amount of water lost each day in New York City by leaky faucets and toilets, is too large a number for first graders to grasp, they could see how drips add up.

Of all the projects and work accomplished during that year, the most significant was our testing of the drinking water in town. In our county, almost all water is drawn from private wells; town water systems do not exist in most communities. Our own town is entirely served by private wells; our school has its own well. New homes, and of course the school, must test their water and prove to the town board of health that it is fit and drinkable. This requirement does not apply to existing homes, and so most of the townspeople do not really know the quality and safety of the water they drink at home, unless they've been willing to pay for expensive tests. Even homes that have been tested are not necessarily safe, as conditions may have changed since the initial test.

As far as we knew, no town with private wells had received a thorough testing of its water. It's an expensive process, and testing is done by the state only in times and specific sites of crisis. We had an opportunity, using students and families, to test the entire town of Shutesbury—not every home, but a sampling of homes spread across every part of town. If there were patterns of contamination or concern, there was a good chance we would catch them.

We established a partnership with an ecology class at Hampshire College in Amherst. Professor John Reid offered to make his laboratory and students available to help us. We could not do a full battery of water tests, due to our limitations of equipment and expertise, so we decided to focus on two areas of particular concern for people in town: lead pollution and sodium pollution.

Lead pollution in drinking water is often caused by the lead solder in the joints of metal pipes leaching into the water supply. Even infinitesimal amounts of lead, fifty parts per billion, represent a serious danger. The more acidic the water, the greater the chance of contamination. With our wells being filled by increasingly acidic rain, many people were getting nervous. Third- and fourth-grade pH readings of local streams and ponds confirmed our fears that our town's water was more acidic than it should be. Sodium pollution can be caused either by natural ground salts, or when the salt that is poured onto icy roads in winter leaches into the soil and ground water. Some areas in town, particularly homes at the base of steep hills, seemed to have good cause for worry. We resolved to test for sodium and lead content, and also to check the acidity of water samples.

We began by holding whole school assemblies. We explained the project, and answered questions. We described artesian wells—how they are dug, why they work, and how they can become endangered. We sent a letter home to each family, inviting them to participate if they felt comfortable doing so. No family refused, and many were anxious to begin. Attached to the letter was a request that each student, or student-parent team, draw a rough map of the location of their well. We asked them to provide an aerial view of the home, road, and well, with approximate distances and slopes indicated. This would enable us to look for a correlation between sodium content and well placement, in case road salt was running downhill into a home's water supply.

John Reid provided sterile sample bottles, two for every child and staff member at the school, and a pile of extras for mistakes. First, Reid taught the sixth-grade students the proper method of drawing water samples. The procedure had to be followed exactly to ensure accuracy. Then the sixth graders held an assembly for the entire school and gave a lesson in proper sampling techniques. They distributed sample kits containing bottles and instructions to every child, kindergarten on up. Students were instructed to take the samples themselves, or to have a parent help. Any mistakes in the procedure, even a single toilet flush during the night, had to be recorded and turned in with the samples, as it might affect the outcome.

At this point, word of the study had gotten around town. The town board of health was in touch; not only were board members anxious to hear the results, but some of them asked if they could have their own wells tested. Requests for tests came from all over—relatives and friends of staff, relatives of students, neighbors of students—everyone wanted their wells tested.

When the samples came in, small groups of fifth- and sixth-grade students brought them down to the Hampshire College laboratory, driven by parent volunteers. In the lab, the fifth and sixth graders were taught to calibrate and run the analysis machines by the college students. While the young students were running the machines under the supervision of the older students, a separate team of fifth and sixth graders videotaped the process with the school's camcorder. Phase 1 of this project, the analysis of samples, was completed in a few days. Fifth and sixth graders then directed an assembly for the whole school where they explained the process to the students and the school staff, using the videotape as part of the lesson. Our next task was to analyze the data—enter the results on town maps, arrange and graph the data to look for trends, and assess the degree of the problem in our town.

Meanwhile, some of us on the staff were starting to panic. Initially, this project seemed like both a great learning experience and a public service; it was perfect. Now the gravity of the project began to sink in. What if some family wells had lead content high enough to present a real danger? Who was going to break the news to the family? If students were in charge of all the data, there was no way to keep such a finding secret, or even guarded. What if property values in town were imperiled by our findings? Could we even trust our findings? Were we liable for any problems we created? We called our town lawyer to discuss these issues.

The students, meanwhile, were buried under reams of computer printouts, working in teams to organize and present the data. Lists and charts were created. The third and fourth grades had drafted an extraordinary town map in the school library to record their water acidity findings, a map that took up an entire wall. We marked the home of every student in the school on the map, and entered the data from the well next to the home. This enabled us to look for neighborhood patterns.

Reporters were coming to the school regularly during this period to get updates on the results. Staff members spoke to them, but told them frankly that if they wanted an appraisal of the data so far they would have to talk to the students. Students were analyzing and interpreting the data; they knew more than staff did at that point. Students even talked on the phone with reporters to give updates.

Luckily for us and for everyone in town, no samples revealed levels of lead or sodium that were clearly dangerous. Some samples were slightly higher than recommended levels, and we requested more samples from these homes so we could retest them. There was a wide range of levels of both contaminants in the samples, and our job now was to try to find patterns and relationships in the data.

John Reid taught the sixth-grade students methods of plotting the data on graphs to examine correlations. We examined the following correlations in graphic form: pH to sodium, well depth to sodium, distance from road to sodium, pH to lead, and sodium to lead. We also examined the relationship of the pH of the first water sample taken in the morning to the second sample, taken after the system had been thoroughly flushed out.

Our findings were interesting, and not what we had predicted. We found no correlation between well depth or placement and sodium levels. There was no evidence that road salt was affecting wells in a substantial manner. Lead levels were acceptable throughout town, but were higher in wells where the water was more acidic. Also, in about a third of the wells, the second water sample was significantly more acidic than the first, indicating that the water had been buffered by sitting in the pipes overnight. Had lead levels been high, this would have suggested that one should run the water in the morning for a few minutes before using any to drink.

These findings were relayed to the school by the students who had prepared the graphs. The students used chart-size versions of these graphs in an assembly to explain to the school their findings, and also to teach younger students how to read such graphs. The findings were also shared with the community and, through newspapers, with neighboring towns. As the use of road salt was a controversial issue throughout the region, our findings held real significance for towns in our area.

Our student scientists felt on top of the world. The work they had accomplished was not only accurate, clear, and elegantly portrayed, but it was important. Not important school work, but important work in the real world. To this day, I'm not sure that any community in the state has more accurate data on possible road salt contamination of wells than these studies prepared by elementary students for the town of Shutesbury. Of course, students wanted to extend and continue the testing work, but the staff declined. We felt as if we had ulcers by now, and thought that some work that was a little less vital would suit us just fine for a while.

Our Shutesbury water study officially ended on a bright, sunny day in June, our second Wyola Day. We loaded into cars—parents, students, and staff—and headed to the lake for a day of research and fun. On this day, the research and projects of students were combined with some less serious lake activities: swimming, boating, volleyball, sand castles, and a whole school picnic. In the same way that the morale and spirit of the staff was nurtured with workshops, trips, and events during this water study, we felt that the morale and spirit of the whole school wouldn't be hurt by a little water fun. What kind of water expedition would it be without bathing suits and splash fights?

10

Truck, Boat, Train, Bus:
A First-Grade Expedition into Transportation

Tammy Duehr and Shari Flatt with Emily Cousins

This chapter grew out of conversations with first-grade teachers Tammy Duehr and Shari Flatt. Duehr and Flatt reflect on teaching a learning expedition on the types of transportation found in and around their home-town. They call attention to the importance of attending closely to children's ideas, using community experts, and employing the process of revision. Flatt and Duehr teach at Table Mound Elementary School in Dubuque, Iowa, a medium-sized city on the banks of the Mississippi River. Situated in the rural Midwest, Dubuque is surrounded by farm and cattle country. The contrasts between modes of transportation—rural and urban, land and water—adds another dimension to the students' inquiry.

Overview

Duehr: When we first decided to do an expedition on transportation, I was a little leery because I didn't know much about the subject. But I knew it would be something the children would be motivated to learn about.

At the beginning of the expedition, I planned for an entire week. Toward the end I began to realize I could rarely plan that far in advance. I found myself always responding to the children's interests—they initiated the direction we went in. A child would ask an important question, and I would drop what I had planned for the day, knowing we could get to it later. Now, a plan for me is not really a plan; it's an idea. That way of thinking is a big change for me. When you make that shift, it means that you—the teacher—are not always the leader. That can be a scary place to find yourself.

We started the expedition by finding out what the students wanted to know. Instead of trying to answer all of their questions ourselves, we brought in community experts.

We broke the expedition down into trucks, cars, planes, boats, and trains. We examined each area for about a week. We tried to begin or end each segment with a community expert. Our major project was building a model city that incorporated all of the modes of transportation we had studied. Aside from a separate time for math and specialists, the rest of the day was spent on the expedition. Each day we began with a morning circle, followed by small-group work. Then we would devote time to literature and writing, usually related to the expedition. Finally, the entire afternoon was focused on projects related to the expedition.

The community experts who came to talk to the students were an important part of the expedition. We explained to the experts that they shouldn't make a formal presentation, but instead should come prepared to answer questions. I had to remind them that my students are six years old—they want to know how heavy things are and how much everything costs. When the students found out that the first mode of transportation we went to see—a semi cab—cost $290,000, we began making graphs to compare the costs of different kinds of transportation.

Flatt: I enjoyed the community experts a great deal. I didn't expect to learn so much from them. Our city planner, Laura Carston, brought in maps of the city, aerial photographs of our school, and the plans for the city over the next five years. She had never done anything like this with small children. The students asked her lots of questions. She talked about how to construct a model of a city, and that gave us ideas for building our own. I especially enjoyed when she asked them, "What does a city need to live and grow?"

Other speakers included a train engineer, truck drivers, a city bus driver, and Coast Guard personnel. You could tell the bus driver had never spoken to a group of children. At first he was shy, but then he warmed up. All three classes piled into his bus, and he drove us around the parking lot. The children were fascinated by the differences between city and school buses.

We also went to a number of transportation-related sites around town. When I called these places to ask if they could give us fifteen minutes of their time, I found myself being apologetic. It wasn't until I looked back and saw how everyone treated us so well that I realized it was as if they had been waiting for years for children to visit. They thought of it as an honor. They said, "We'd love to have your class come. We already have an idea of what we'd like to do with them." Sometimes we even found businesses that had programs already set up for children, but no one had ever asked for their help. I began to realize I didn't have to be apologetic.

The Project: Model Cities

Duehr: I explained to the children that we were going to make a model city. They had no idea what that meant, and neither did I! It was awkward when they asked, "What do you mean we're making a city?" and I had to answer, "I don't know." I felt uncomfortable with that answer, but I'm getting better at admitting what I don't know. They're getting better too, because they no longer expect me to know everything. It was hard to start the day when I was unsure where it was going to end. Of course that can also be exciting, because you have nothing when you start, but by the end of the day the children have done so much.

When our team of teachers talked about building a model city, we had something small in mind—ten houses all in a row and miniature dogs. The children, however, were thinking big—painted boxes and planes on spirals flying in the air. I couldn't believe what they came up with! At points I had to stop myself from saying, "This is not what I had in mind." I had to let go. In the end they created something far better than anything I had imagined.

Every day, we worked on our major project—the model city. The model's purpose was to show how the modes of transportation are related. We started by talking about what structures and forms of transportation should be included in our cities. One day, after eating oranges for lunch, I asked, "Where does our lunch come from? How did these oranges come to Dubuque in autumn?" The first things they mentioned were those we had already been studying—an airport, a boat dock, a train station. Then I asked the children some questions to draw out their thinking, such as "Where does the food go once it comes off the truck?"

Flatt: I divided the children into seven cooperative groups. We made one city, but each group worked on a section of it. First, they decided on the sections they wanted their city to have—a downtown, a mall, a factory, and so forth. Then they chose the section they wanted to work on.

Duehr: In my class, there were only two sections, mostly because of space considerations. First the children made maps of the city. Before we put anything down on the board, we drew roads. Then the children painted the roads. They painted one yellow because it was a farm road, then went outside to get dirt and let it dry on the paint so it looked authentic.

Flatt: Each day, you could tell they had been thinking about the project since the previous day, because when they got together in their cooperative groups they were instantly engaged. They remembered the problems they had encountered from the previous day, and they had ideas about how to solve them.

Duehr: And there were lots of problems to solve: how to put up the buildings, how to support them so they wouldn't fall down. Where should the windows go? Who should paint which buildings? They worked well together in small groups. My role was to help them when they got stuck.

One of the skills the students developed was planning ahead. We asked them, "What do you want to do tomorrow? If you want blue paint, you need to let me know." We had a system where the children put a list of the things they needed for the next day in my mailbox. One day there was a request for a softball. I wondered what in the world they wanted a softball for, but I went ahead and got it for them. The next day the children made a water tower out of it. After a certain point I stopped asking questions and got them whatever they requested.

There was one thing I thought they did backward, but I didn't say anything. First the students made a map of the city, then immediately they put the boxes representing the buildings on. I remember thinking it would have been much easier to start by laying down the surface textures, like grass and tarmac, so they wouldn't have to work around the buildings, but I didn't say anything. I told the other teachers, "How am I going to stop the children from doing this? They are going to get to a point where they're frustrated, and I'm going to have to step in and do it for them. So why don't I just tell them now?" But I didn't say anything, even though it was hard to be silent.

The students got the buildings up, but they still didn't see the problem. The city looked finished to them. But there was still no grass or plant life; everything was brown cardboard. I kept wondering how I could communicate this to them. One day I decided to read aloud a book that would suggest the idea of grass. As I was reading it, all of a sudden one child shouted, "We don't have any grass in our city!"

Now the group had to figure out how to get some plant life in their model. At first they wanted me to figure it out. They asked me what I thought they should do, but I encouraged them to come up with their own ideas. So they decided to use Easter grass, but there was nowhere to get it, this being Christmastime. So one of the children brought in an artificial garland from his Christmas tree. I thought, "This is going to be interesting, because the grass will be higher than the buildings." But then they squeezed glue all over the cardboard, then cut the garland and let it fall. It looked better than if I had done it myself.

Something similar happened with the flood wall. At first they wanted it to be taller than the highest building, but that's not how tall Dubuque's flood wall is. I tried to bring them as much information as I could, but I didn't want to tell them everything. I was walking a fine line, because I didn't want them constructing something that didn't make sense. Before they glued their walls on, I suggested they go to the flood wall. They came back the next day, looked at their model and said, "It's not that tall; we walked on it."

One group used a cereal box for their hospital. We were using water-based paints, so every time they tried to paint it, the paint peeled off. This happened three times before I said, "Do you think maybe we should figure out another way?" They remembered that paint stuck to masking tape, so instead of getting a new box that didn't have a shiny finish, they put masking tape around the entire box and painted it.

Later I told them, "You discovered all by yourself that the paint wouldn't stick to the box's surface." They all looked at me in shock and got very upset. "You knew all along it wouldn't stick to the box!" I explained that I enjoyed watching them figure it out on their own. I think I have grown a lot as a teacher by letting them discover on their own.

Flatt: Our cities turned out very differently. Now when I read our expedition plan, I know why. It says, "The class will plan a model city on paper, incorporating all modes of transportation. Students will collect and make materials as needed." Talk about open-ended! "Lay out a city on a 4-by-8 foot sheet of particleboard. Use the cooperative groups to make the model. Models will be displayed and explained at the exhibition." This is the first time we've done a learning expedition; it's the first time the children have done one. We're all bound to learn from it.

As we do more expeditions, my view of what a project is has changed. The word project seems to imply big. I was a little intimidated by that. Now I realize that a big project is made up of a lot of smaller ones. For example, doing multiple drafts is part of a project. Now we do rough drafts automatically. One child finished a project, but she was not satisfied with it. We circled up and I said, "I'm getting the feeling that some of you who are done are not happy with your work. What do you think we should do?" One of the students said, "I know, we should start over, and get another piece of good paper even though we've already done one copy." Before too long they were saying, "You can't just copy it over on good paper. You have to do another draft and then do a final one on good paper."

Peer Critique and the Process of Revision

Duehr: We have put a lot of work into revision. We tell the children we don't want them to do another copy; it has to be a draft that is better, or somehow different. We talked about how to critique, about how they shouldn't say, "That's really stupid." They shouldn't laugh at each other. The students started each critique session by saying three things they liked about the piece of work. Then they followed up by adding ideas about how the author could improve his or her work. It took a long time for them not to say, "That doesn't look like a bird." Now they're at a point where they say, "I really like your bird nest. Are there eggs in it?" The artist might reply, "No, that's the dad bird, so I don't want any eggs in there."

My students are organized into teams of two or three. When they create something, they are supposed to critique it first with someone in their group. It's their responsibility to seek someone out. When they come to me to get a final piece of paper, I ask, "With whom did you critique?"

The process of revision has added hours of effort to the projects. They put so much time into their work now that they're proud of it. When I compare what we are doing this year with other years, I realize I'm not doing everything I used to do. But when I ask myself if we're getting to the content, the answer is always, "Yes."

I've seen the quality of their work go sky-high. They are becoming better writers. We have a pattern established for creating good work, and my children know how to go through the steps of revision. When I articulate high expectations, they really respond. Their attitude has changed to the point where they will try anything.

Flatt: All of their drafts were useful for assessment, but the most important were the final products—the books the students wrote about each mode of transportation. When they began reading each other's books and struggling with the vocabulary, I had plenty of opportunities to assess their reading, vocabulary, and comprehension. I saw what they learned about each mode of transportation. Also, we started teaching skills and vocabulary by using their own writing. They read each other's books. A child might say, "I can't read Eric's book because it has ten sentences on a page and that's too much." So I would reply, "Well, maybe with Eric's help you could read it."

Duehr: I found that most of the children were successful at reading their own books. But they became an effective assessment tool when the children read each other's because they weren't reading from memory. We asked each of the students to read his or her own book into a tape recorder. We would like to use this recording next year as a benchmark for them, as a way to discuss their progress and their goals for the new year.

We found we had to start thinking about assessment as soon as we began the expedition. The expectations have to be right up front for the students, so we—as teachers—need to think about them from the beginning. We put them out there before the children begin working on something. As we went through the expedition, we began to realize the importance of developing expectations with students. For the children's books, the teachers established the expectations. But with the model city, there was a lot more discussion with the students of what the city should look like. As a result, all ninety books from the three classes were similar, and all three model cities looked dramatically different.

Clear standards are very helpful for instilling in students an ability to self-assess. They have been crucial in getting students to be their own leaders because they see what's expected of them. When they begin a project, they know what components they need to include. If they don't get the maximum number of points, they realize it's not because the teacher doesn't like them or because they didn't have any choices. When it comes to the actual learning, my role stops and theirs begins. I tell them that even at this age, they have to be responsible for their learning.

There is more pressure to perform when the whole class sets up the expectations, because then it's not just a matter of letting yourself or the teacher down, but it's the whole class. I think that's part of why there is more success. Making the expectations clear is new for me. I always knew what the expectations were, and maybe I thought I was conveying them, but now I leave no room for doubt. Now they know what's expected, because not only have I said it aloud, but I've also put it in writing.

Design Principles

Duehr: Talking about Expeditionary Learning's design principles helps me as much as it helps the students. We usually do it before we start an expedition so we know where we're headed. We also talk about these principles whenever something happens during the day that exemplifies one of them.

They see better than I do how competition and collaboration fit together. They know that competition means trying to do better, but they also know how important collaboration is since they are accustomed to working in cooperative groups. We do a lot of competitive games with math, both as individuals and with groups. They talk about competition in physical education, but I want them to see it in relation to other things as well. Similarly, I want them to see how all the other design principles occur within P.E.

Once when we were discussing the design principles, one student said he had observed Intimacy and Caring at work in the class, but another student disagreed. He said, "I had my feelings hurt a lot during this expedition. I agreed to have my building painted brown, but I still wanted it painted blue." He wanted us to know he could live with the decision, but he wasn't sure that the children who painted it brown really cared about his opinion. I think we were all pleased that he felt he could bring his feelings to the group.

When I think of Solitude and Reflection, I think of writing. I had some children who couldn't read and write, and I wondered how I was going to encourage them to reflect. So this year I start each class with an opening and closing circle. I think it's important to give children something to focus on during reflection time, otherwise they might not understand what they're supposed to be doing. So we came up with the idea of posing questions that the children could sit quietly and think about, but not answer aloud. We asked the students to think about the day—what they were proud of, and what they might do differently. Sometimes I framed the question by asking them what they would tell their parents they did in school that day. Also, the projects provided a good source of reflection, because I could ask them if they had met their goals for the day.

Now they're so accustomed to reflecting that as soon as I say, "Circle up," they sit down and close their eyes. They know not to talk, and they don't look to anyone else because they are too busy thinking to themselves. There are times when I tell them reflection time is over, and they say, "Wait, I'm not done yet."

Flatt:　At first I thought my children would be too young for reflection. The silence seemed to last an eternity. I had to count to ten and say, "No one can raise their hand until I snap my fingers." Even for me, ten seconds of silence seemed very long. Now they are comfortable with a minute or two. It took time to build up to that. I see it as a way of teaching them to think on their own. Some of my children need to focus on what it actually means to think about something. I try to model different types of reflection, so they realize that reflection means more than simply thinking about one's feelings. For instance, I keep a journal, and I read from it sometimes.

Duehr:　One of the things that strengthens reflection in my classroom is community circle. Ritual is a big part of it. It's the best vehicle for my students to communicate about problems they're experiencing. We don't raise our hands in community circle because it seems forced. Instead, when we want to talk, we put our hands on our knees, which is a less obtrusive form of communication. I always ask them how they feel about things that come up in class. I try to draw them out. If they say, "I feel bad," I will ask, "Well, what do you mean when you say 'bad'?" I encourage them to verbalize.

Flatt: My children love community circle, too. Now they come to me and say, "I think we need to circle up." The physical shape of the circle was something we had to work on. A circle allows everyone to look at each other, but at first they wanted to look at me the whole time. So in the beginning, I took myself out of the circle and sat behind. I didn't really like doing that, because I wanted to be considered part of the group, but it was the only way to get them to talk to one another. We have rules for when we are in a circle. We have to hold still, our eyes are on the speaker, and we are quiet. All of those things add up to being a good listener. We just kept practicing them over and over again.

Duehr: They know there are not going to be negative consequences for expressing themselves. Of course at first they used bad language, and I had to say, "I know we said you could say anything you want, but I think you know that's inappropriate." They'll test every rule until they feel the parameters of where they can go.

What we build together in our community circle is felt throughout the day. They can speak directly to one another through the circle, and they know they can do it in a safe way. I encourage them to go as far as they can on their own in resolving their problems. If they really can't solve the problem, I'll intervene. But we haven't had any big problems so far, and that tells me it's working. It has taken time for the children who are new to get used to all this. I have had children who are new to my class approach my desk to tell me something, and another child will stop them and say, "I'll talk to you about it."

The Culminating Exhibition

Duehr: We wanted to celebrate all the hard work we had done on the model cities, so we planned a big exhibition at the end of the expedition. Usually when you think of a school presentation, you think of people in rows of folding chairs, overheads, and pulling the children in front of a microphone to sing a song. At first, that's what we had in mind. But once we saw the quality of work the students had created, we realized a staged presentation would not do it justice. The quality of the work drove the chairs away. There was no way the excitement and accomplishment of ninety children were going to be conveyed on stage. We decided we wanted to have tables full of the children's books, drawings, and stories. But we found that if there were tables then there wouldn't be enough room for lines of chairs. So the idea of displaying student work and letting them show it off seemed like the best way to go.

I really enjoyed seeing the children take their parents by the hand and interact with their work. They read them their books, walked them through the model city, showed them the literature and graphs of data, and told them their stories. Many parents had expressions on their faces that said, "I can't believe my child knows all of this!" I think what was most impressive was the depth of the children's knowledge, and the integrated quality of it. The work showed that the children had a grasp of how transportation operates within a city.

The walls were plastered with artwork and posters that demonstrated the progression from earlier drafts to final ones. Parents could follow a student's work through all the drafts, which said so much more about revision than anything we could have told them. We posted the skills we had focused on, because we wanted parents to know that the children were engaged academically. But other than that, the teachers didn't have much to do. The children were the facilitators. They did all the talking. If I had done the work, I would have been busy showing it to people, but this was the students' work. I didn't do much more than smile the entire evening.

11

Are We There Yet? Immersion Journalism as a Discussion of Good Work

Connie Russell-Rodriguez with Javier Mendez,
Marie Keem, and Dennie Palmer Wolf

In this chapter, Connie Russell-Rodriguez and her partner, Javier Mendez, lead their students on an expedition into the varieties and history of social activism. Students use "immersion journalism," where they shadow activists and record scenes from their lives, to study local people who strive to improve the quality of life of their community. Along the way, they examine the work of Americans throughout history who have made a stand to help others. Russell-Rodriguez also describes how she enables students to excel through providing opportunities for them to revisit and revise their work, and by putting concrete models of excellence, and discussions about the qualities of good work, at the center of her classroom.

Our Signature: Activism

My school, the Rafael Hernandez, is a kindergarten–eighth-grade school near Egleston Square in Boston. The Hernandez is a two-way bilingual school where students develop both English and Spanish as academic languages throughout kindergarten–eighth grades. Every classroom contains both native English and Spanish speakers who come primarily from families with low incomes. Approximately 40 percent of students receive some form of special education. The middle school contains approximately eighty students from sixth through eighth grades. The school is situated a neighborhood that many would call "tough," even "dangerous." However, in the last decade, the neighborhood has been turning the quality of life around, thanks to the hard work and dedication of a linked group of neighborhood agencies. One of the original schools involved in the Expeditionary Learning design, the Hernandez has been working with a view of learning as a sustained journey into new territories of understanding. This work has also been an expedition (or several rolled into one) for teachers as much as for students. In this process, we have had to ask one another hard questions about what counts as quality. Thus, in all these respects, our students, families, community, and faculty all know what it is to fight toward quality, even against the odds.

As a result, our work has its own stamp or signature. Several expeditions (and also much of the way we talk and teach) focused on the theme of activism, or the study of how individuals act on behalf of their peoples and communities to secure a better life. When we first introduce the topic of activism, students immediately think of monumental figures like Cesar Chavez or Malcolm X, but we also want them to study and appreciate the familiar individuals and organizations in their own community that refuse to let things be as they have always been. Therefore, while our expeditions are rooted in the history of well-known individuals and historical movements, we have long insisted that they include studies of living individuals who are active in neighborhood and city life. This springs from our belief that particularly in the challenging, even harsh urban environments where our students become young adults, they cannot afford to grow up as victims or passive subjects. They—and their families—need an activists energy, resiliency, and generosity, especially now, when so much of what my students hear about immigrants and non-English speakers is selfish, even full of hatred.

The notion of "immersion journalism" provided the spark to bring these two strands—the concern for creating a culture of excellence and the urgent need for activism—together. We were in the middle of rethinking about how to make the mandatory eighth-grade study of American history into a series of linked expeditions—ones that were more than an excursion along the Freedom Trail or a visit to Plymouth Rock. So often my students are puzzled about why they should study "people back then." They want to know why history matters, especially when most of the materials available to us say little about the lives of people who were not English speakers, and not members of the mainstream culture. I saw in immersion journalism the first glimmers of how we could continue to emphasize the constructive role of activism, connect "then" and "now," and move our classroom conversations steadily toward talking about the kind of excellent work that will make it possible for my students to belong, take part, and speak out.

Making a Difference

We designed an expedition, "Making a Difference," that was focused on Americans throughout history who have decided to take a stand on behalf of others. We knew we wanted to publish a magazine that would discuss what it takes to become an American brave enough to take a stand and to act on it—despite personal cost. Like all our expeditions, it has already had a long and evolving life. We originally taught it for the first time in the spring of 1995. We revised and retaught it again the following fall.

In both rounds, the first portion of this expedition found us deep in the history of the Americas. Working with materials from North, Central, and South America, our students studied the lives of people who elected to make a difference. In all cases, we worked across multiple sources of information: history textbooks, historical documents, historical fiction, and film in order to build up a complex picture of both the conditions and the choices that lie behind activists' work. The students began by reading a biography of Harriet Tubman which we chose specifically because it included a timeline that cross-referenced the events in Tubman's life with other simultaneous historical events. Thus, an individual heroine was placed in the context of earlier developments, specifically, the wider effort to end slavery and the lives of other participants in that effort. The book also provided us with a first chance to urge excellence. We created a companion activity book/journal designed to prompt all students to think not only about the obvious aspects of reading comprehension, but also about the sources and significance of Harriet Tubman's life and actions as an activist. In this way, we tried to ensure that everyone had the basis for joining in class discussions. We were also trying to stress that a command of information and a hold on the details was vital. Students would never be strong journalists if they couldn't get the facts down. The result was that we had much more vigorous and searching conversations in class. Classroom discussion, even of topics as demanding as the role of singing in enslaved communities began to have this kind of energy and detail:

STUDENTS: It was the only thing they could do. It was like praying.
CONNIE: Did they sing, "I hate my master, I want to be free!"?
STUDENT: They talked about following the river.
CONNIE: The word I'm going for is *symbolic*. There were a lot of references to Moses. What could Moses mean to them?
STUDENT: Someone was coming to take them out of bondage.
CONNIE: Harriet Tubman became known as Moses, even if people didn't know her real name . . . What about "follow the drinking gourd"?
(As the discussion continues, students work out that the drinking gourd is a symbolic name for the Big Dipper, the constellation containing the North Star, that escaping slaves could follow to freedom.)

Before moving on to a new section, the students wrote their thoughts in the reflections section. This regularly occurring reflections page allowed students to respond in their own style and according to their own thoughts: some drew pictures depicting scenes in Harriet Tubman's life, while others summarized the chapter, and still others compared their own experiences with Harriet Tubman's or speculated on how they would react in her position. Here we were trying to guarantee that everyone had the chance to think about the large questions at stake, not just the definition of the term *abolitionist*. For us, this kind of practice in discussing large questions was an absolutely necessary foundation for being able to take on the journalism assignment that would culminate the expedition.

In the next portion of the expedition, students acted together as a research community. Each one had to read and conduct research in order to produce two kinds of writing. The first was a review of a book or a film that they had used in their research. Students had the option of writing this review for either an English- or a Spanish-speaking audience. The point is that both languages have the power to communicate personal vision, large ideas, and reflections on history.

A Time for Justice
by Alexander Reyes

"A Time for Justice" is a video which informs people about what condition we were in, with the violence that had been occurring, during the years before the Civil Rights movement. The violence, destruction, and taking of lives had happened many years ago. Yes, these negative occurrences continue to happen (now) as they did years ago.

This video is just a reminder of what are the changes that have happened since the civil rights movement began, and about the violence that has been happening during the past years.

Harriet Tubman
by Miozoty Vega

Yo leí el libro Harriet Tubman *por Ann Petry, una historia sobre una extraordinaría mujer llamada Harriet Tubman. Le llamo extraordinaría por la vida que vivió. Ayudó a los esclavos librarse de la vida horrible que llevaban.*

Harriet hizo diecinueve viajes hasta el sur para ayudar escapar a los esclavos. Todos sus viajes fueron largos, peligrosos, calurosos, y muy cansadores, pero ella nunca descanso hasta tener su familia en libertad. Aunque era peligrosa lo que ella hacía, no dejaba que el miedo le paralizara . . .

I read the book Harriet Tubman by Ann Petry, a history about an extraordinary woman named Harriet Tubman. I call her extraordinary because of the life she lived. She helped slaves free themselves from the horrible lives they had to live.

Harriet made nineteen trips to the south to help slaves escape. All her trips were long, dangerous, hot and tiring, but she never rested until she delivered her family to freedom. Although what she did was dangerous, she never let fear paralyze her.

Students also wrote a short, summary biography of a person who had made a difference: Shirley Chisholm, Thurgood Marshall, Cesar Chavez, and others. Because Javier, my coteacher, is a Colombian with vivid memories of participating in one of the many student revolutions of the 1960s and 1970s, we were able to bring a deliberately pan-American perspective to our historical work. Students studied and wrote about figures like Luis Muñoz Marín and Rigoberta Menchú right along side of Marshall and Chavez.

In many cases we were pleased. At least for a beginning. Students appeared to be "getting" several important ideas. The first was that their biographies moved—at least a few steps—away from paragraphs copied straight out of the encyclopedia. Students understood, at least to some degree, that they were meant to be explaining the conditions, selecting the high points, and making an evaluation of the key choices that that person had made. Also, we began to see the first hints of writing that didn't plod—words and phrases that caught some of the fire of those individual brave choices. These pieces, when they were finally assembled, gave us the section of our publication "Activists in History."

With this as background we were ready to move toward our immersions in the lives of current-day activists. But not without first building the tools students needed. An important part of immersion journalism is becoming aware of intimate details that help paint the scene, and that turn the writer into someone who has an inside perspective to relate to the reader. This means being very observant. To get into this idea, we had someone observe our class and type up notes for the students to look at. They thought she was incredibly nosy, but we pointed out that she had gotten down a lot of good details. Here are her notes:

Activity: Watching video about the Civil Rights movement
Situation: Lights are out, the shades are down, everyone is quiet and watching the video. There is not much other movement.
General observations:
■ *There are twenty students in the room.*

- *The bulletin board across from me has a purple background. The only thing on the board is a sheet of paper from a large pad which says*
  Rubric for Descriptive Writing
  1. Use descriptive adjectives
  2. Include details
  3. Use verbs that show action
- *To the left of the sheet with writing on it hangs the whole pad of blank sheets.*
- *J. is turned to the window. Another boy is also turned to the window.*
- *F. is writing something. There is violence on the screen and she looks up, then looks back to her paper. At the same time a couple of the boys exchange words.*
- *S. is looking in her notebook and flipping through the pages. She doesn't look up.*
- *A couple of other girls are working on other papers.*
- *Connie is standing directly across from the TV, leaning against the heater, with her eyes looking straight at the screen.*
- *Two girls in front of me are having a quiet conversation.*

Shortly after that we started our own observations. Students went in pairs to another classroom at the Hernandez, where they observed for fifteen minutes, then they came back with their observations and talked about everything that they had written down. The follow-up was to write their observations in a story format for which we talked about using descriptors and interesting verbs to tell the story of what they saw. In order to provide a model and a basis for discussion of how the transition from notes to a story occurs, I took the earlier notes from the outside observer and wrote a story based on them:

Write-up

"Rubrics for Descriptive Writing" is what meets my eye as I walk in. It is a fairly spacious room with the desks arranged in pairs and about twenty students of various shades. They are watching a movie, and some of them are interested, yet some seem less so. Is it that the movie isn't interesting, or do they have their minds filled with other, more pressing problems?

The teacher is in the back of the room, eyes on the television and apparently engrossed in the movie. Beside her a distracted boy turns toward the window. The shade is down . . . what could he be looking at?

We then listened to an interview called "A Boy's Shelter for Street People" from a taped National Public Radio program. We wanted the students to think about asking good questions, but the content was too absorbing to pick apart for technique.

Even so, students were able to hear how the interviewer's open-ended questions pushed the interaction along and made the story more complex. Building on this, we set up a mock interview and asked two students to take on the role of the interviewer: one was to be an attentive person interested in getting at the interviewee's story, the other was to be a poor interviewer. It worked remarkably well. What emerged is that while our students had had a difficult time listing the qualities of a strong and poor interview, they *could* get these qualities into their performances. For instance, the poor interviewer was distracted, playing with his pencil and staring off into space. The observing students immediately picked up on what they admired in the good interviewer and generated a list of characteristics that we used throughout the remaining portions of our journalism expedition:

A Good Interviewer

maintains eye contact
talks clearly
is observant
is friendly
shows interest
is curious
is flexible
asks good questions
looks for stories

We drove these points home when we invited Mel King, a well-known and very active local figure, to speak to us. Ahead of time, we brainstormed questions based on the fact that Mel King was active in politics in Boston and that he had run for mayor. King is a very quietly charismatic person; he doesn't walk into the room and blow you away. Yet, in part because of their new interest in being interviewers, the students all listened closely as Mr. King spoke for about forty-five minutes, talking about his history as a Boston-based activist. The students did the interview at the very end. We videotaped the interview and that let us review what happened. When we watched it with the cool eyes of observers and critics, many students heard King preface several of his answers with phrases such as "Like I said before . . ." Instantly, they recognized that he was signaling that he thought he had already given this information. In those few minutes, virtually every eighth grader learned about the importance of using a list of questions flexibly. This is evident even in a short sample of the classroom dialogue that followed:

> CONNIE: Okay, so what does it mean to be flexible in your questioning?
> STUDENT: You have other questions.
> CONNIE: Is going through your list and asking every question being flexible? When might you not want to ask a question?
> STUDENT VOICES: When a speaker has already covered it.

We also went after what *exactly* they meant when they said that an interviewer asks good questions:

> CONNIE: So what is a good question?
> STUDENT: They make sense and have to do with what you know.
> STUDENT: They are open-ended.
> CONNIE: What is open-ended?
> STUDENT: It takes more than one word to answer.
> CONNIE: Give me an example.
> STUDENT: Why do you like . . .
> CONNIE: Or "Tell me a story from when . . ." Stories are what help you know people.

Having done this careful work with tools, we were as ready as we could be for the next phases in our expedition. In the first excursion, students went on a scavenger hunt that took them throughout Boston. They had to put their observation skills to work: finding locations, monuments, plaques—even a restaurant in Chinatown where they could eat as inexpensively as possible. The expedition included working in a soup kitchen serving dinner. As with any expedition, this one contained not only the inevitable organizational frustrations, but totally unforeseen events that teach in ways it would have been impossible to plan. In this case it was an unexpected interview in which students learned about getting beneath the surface of expectations and stereotypes. A student's account portrays this clearly:

Food Not Bombs

When we got to Food Not Bombs, we were greeted with lots of smiling faces from other volunteers. Food Not Bombs is a completely volunteer organization that makes food and serves it to the homeless . . . Before we got there we all went thinking that the homeless were living in the streets because they did something wrong. I went expecting to feed the homeless. I never expected to get to know them and become their friend.

Some of the people were living on the streets because of reasons like they had just left an abusive relationship and they had nowhere to go and no one to turn to, or other things such as they lost their jobs and had no way to pay mortgage or rent, or they got into an argument with their spouse and their spouse kicked them out of the house.

As I finished serving one homeless woman, an older guy with short blond- and gray-streaked hair, who was also homeless, walked up to me and put a crooked smile on his face. I dropped my hands down to my sides and looking into his dead, dead bluish green cat eyes. I froze for a moment; my eyes seemed to be turning a dark devil's red as tears slowly began rolling down my face.

He took a clean napkin, wiped my tears, and tried to comfort me. He told me that it was okay to cry and he had tears, too. His eyes started to bulge, I could see his veins in his head, and tears began to run down his cheeks as he told me how he became homeless. He was a veteran in the army. When he got back to America after Vietnam he had no home, no family, nowhere to go, and no money. He had no choice but to go to a shelter or live on the streets . . .

This trip has changed my thoughts about the homeless and helping my community more. I hope that this article has changed your thoughts about the homeless and has encouraged you to help your community. I hope you know what you have is luxurious compared to some of the things that other people have and that you should appreciate it.

— Ebony Williams

Immersion Experiences

After the urban exploration, it was time for the students to go out individually and to step into the lives of local activists, spending a day at work shadowing them. They had spent hours ahead of time talking with and contacting people they thought might be interested. Finally, they had a list of people at community health services, educational centers, and so forth.

Going to places and asking questions and interviewing turned out to have been a very effective dress rehearsal for our students. Even though they were anxious when they went out to spend a full day with an individual, they were brave and competent—most children came back with as many as six pages of notes. They all had had different experiences, but no one was disappointed. Except perhaps the teachers. Those half-dozen pages of notes that the students returned with were full of the facts—but that is all. The bare bones were present—but little insight, and no sense of character.

We were lucky, however. We had scheduled students to visit someone for one day and then visit for a follow-up day a week later—which was good foresight. It was obvious when we talked after the first day that the whole process of shadowing, interviewing, and creating a profile of an unusual individual wasn't at all clear to students. Also, students didn't get anywhere near the information they needed to be able to write it up as we wanted.

We also went through an article about Tom Cruise that had appeared in *Life* magazine. Every time something was communicated, we asked, "Okay, now which is that?" and said, "Okay, the interviewer must have asked for that piece of information because there's no other way she would know that with asking." Then there were other things: how he was dressed, how far down his shirt was unzipped, and so forth. Obviously you don't have to ask somebody, "Excuse me, can I measure that?" That's observation. As we did that, we said, "This is how we want your write-ups to be, a combination. We want you to mix observation, the interview questions, and quotes so that you get a real feel for the person." And we talked a little bit with the students about style. We pointed out that in the Tom Cruise article all the sentences were short and choppy, and the prose was fast, and in a couple of places the author actually says, "He's a very fast character." So we talked about the congruency between style and the personality the author was describing. As we ended the discussion of the Tom Cruise article, a couple of students said, "Well, I don't know that information about my person!" and our reply was, "Well, that's why you're going back on Wednesday!" Until they had focused access to concrete examples of how other writers pieced together their portraits, students simply thought their job was to write up a description of the person's *job,* not of the person as someone whose history and experiences drew him or her into making change in the community. With this new understanding in mind, we created a web of questions for the second round of interviewing and observation. These questions were hugely different from the simple name, age, salary inquiries that students had begun by using. Now students wanted to know about the person's childhood, life as a young adult, and what drew him or her to activism. The results appeared in the section entitled "The Faces of Activism in Boston." In the end, these portraits let us see the clothes, the offices, and the hearts and minds of a wide cross-section of the people working in health care, teen programs, and shelters. Looking over these interviews as a teacher, I am proudest of the fact that you can really see the results of students' having learned to interview: to ask questions, to listen to the answers, to pick out critical quotes, and to reflect on what they have heard. An excerpt from Edson Jean's interview of Darren Clark shows this quality of give and take:

> *Darren Clark decided to work in Dimock because he wanted to work with young people in the community. It's important for young people in the community to see a positive Black man doing something productive that benefits them.*
>
> *Darren has been working at Dimock for three years. In fact, this year is going to be his fourth . . . He used to work in the Department of Youth Services and from there he worked at an alternative school where he was the chief executive officer (CEO).*
>
> *In Darren's opinion, the government is not building schools anymore, they are building jails. Many kids are going to jail at early ages, and cops don't dress like cops; most of them are undercover. That's why it's important for us young kids to get a productive education to become successful adults. He thinks that we don't have to go to college to be a successful person, but I told him that I, Edson Jean, am looking forward to going to college. "You are a very well-thought young man," he said to me, "because having knowledge is the basis of surviving."*

The writing mattered, no question. But it is also true that there were personal effects that went way beyond literacy. Reflecting on these effects, it is clear that the students who were influenced were the ones who had the strongest role models or who were really well matched with their mentor. For example, one student spent the field days with a young man who does outreach to students in gangs. He left a deep imprint on the student especially since the man had been out on the streets and not doing wise things when he was younger. His honesty was stunning. As a teacher, I was very affected by reading what my students wrote about taking for granted their own circumstances. Considering that we look at these students as "at risk, underprivileged," whatever, to have them saying, "Wow, I'm so lucky I have all these things," was really eye-opening.

Reflections: Our Own and Theirs

Finally, students wrote a personal reflection that looked back either on their immersion experience or on the expedition as a whole. These reflections took the form of letters to the editor, which seemed much more in line with our commitment to activism. In many respects, for our students, these kinds of public writings will be critical for the well-being of their communities. But in looking over these reflections, what you see is how often an intensely personal experience turns out to be the key to understanding what lies at the heart of activism. Madelyn Aponte's piece, thinking back to her meetings with homeless people, makes this clear:

> One thing that I was really grateful for was serving breakfast to the homeless at the Boston Common. Yes, I know that I cried a lot, and people might think it was stupid, but it was that I first got butterflies and then I had a feeling that I never got before inside my heart. I was proud that I did what I did for the homeless. But I just can't understand why some people couldn't get it in their heads that what I felt was a feeling I never had before.

> One thing I realized was that, yes, at first it was stupid, but if you understood the feeling that I had inside my heart you'd know that it was just too painful to understand it or explain it . . .

> One of the men came to talk to Ebony and me, telling us that crying was okay, that crying wasn't against the law and if you want to cry just to get your tears or feelings out it was okay. He also told us that crying was something natural and there was nothing wrong with crying. When this nice man told this to Ebony and me, I felt pretty good because this small talk put a smile on my face and because I felt like someone understood why and how I felt.

> —Madelyn Aponte

When we do this expedition again, it will change just as radically as it did in the first revision. If we want writing that takes your heart out or drives home a point, then it cannot happen in eight weeks. That was only enough time for students who were already good writers. But the students who are still playing catch-up never had the chance to get past writing dry, detailed narratives. So are we there yet? No. But like the activists we studied, we are determined to make a difference.

12

Making the Circle Bigger:
A Journey in the South Bronx

Susan McCray

The following chapter describes the experiences of Susan McCray, a teacher and Outward Bound instructor, while working at South Bronx High School. The course she taught integrated experiential learning with a social studies and English curriculum. The class met daily for a double period, and the alumni of the classes formed an Outward Bound club that gathered regularly after school. The school is located in Mott Haven, a section of the Bronx in New York City, and services the local community, whose population is primarily Puerto Rican and Dominican, with a growing number from other Latin American countries, and a small percentage of African Americans. McCray, a white woman, grew up three subway stops and fifteen minutes away on the Upper East Side of Manhattan. "Ironically, the closer I became to these young people," she writes, "the more profoundly aware I became of what I had not experienced in my own life, and of just how far those three subway stops and that fifteen minutes are." The tragic slaying of a young person and the feelings of anger and grief surrounding his death launch a student-driven project to foster a greater sense of community in their school and the surrounding neighborhood by building a park on the theme of hope and unity. "Making the circle bigger" became the vision that united the students.

I will never forget the day we sat on the floor of Room 423. The morning after one of our students, Manny Pichardo, was murdered outside of the school, there was a paralyzing haze of grief, anger, and disbelief hanging over the whole school community. Students and staff floated aimlessly through the halls. Manny, a sweet, well-liked senior, was walking with friends past the corner when the Cypress Gang chose to vent its anger on the local Dominicans. Somebody said something to somebody's girlfriend that offended somebody, and now this seventeen-year-old is another statistic to add to the documentation of the decline of the inner city.

The only force guiding us through the day was that of routine. We gathered as usual, but when class started I asked Garfield, one of my students, to suggest to the others what he had suggested to me. He leaned his long neck forward and gently asked the group if they would push the desks and chairs aside, sit in a circle on the floor, and get real close: "Just like when we were in the woods." As if trapped in slow motion, the room began to transform itself. The only audible sound was that of metal desk and chair legs screeching across the formica floor. As we settled in, some lingered in their seats, and I assured them that no one needed to say or do anything he or she did not want to. Eventually we were still again. I noticed that the cold of the floor under my legs contrasted with the warmth of the shoulders next to me. Suddenly, an array of images and stories came flooding into the room. Kathy hesitantly told of finding a baby in her incinerator. Hector talked of running from bullets. Michelle sadly described going straight home every day after school and never going out.

The conversation reached a low, and then turned. I asked them what could help, and as a group they began to express the feelings of support, trust, and caring they had initially developed during our weekend backpacking trip. Garfield reminded us of what we now call the "Battle of Tiorotti Circle," named for that place midway through our wilderness experience where he was ready to give up and walk away from us.

"But, we talked it out. It sounds so simple," he observed.

Hilda added, "We must hang on to these connections."

Knowing that the bell was about to ring and that we would be forced to leave this secure place, we rose until standing with our arms around each other, and as if on cue Garfield asked the simple question, "How can we make the circle bigger?" Making the circle bigger became our mission; it became the vision that drove us and united us.

Later that day, after school, many students from both the class and club gathered spontaneously to continue their discussion. After returning to the issues and struggles, they soon moved to brainstorming and planning. Carmen suggested that they become the unity task force of the school. Joey thought they could call themselves "United As One," and reach out to all students through peer counseling and student government. Geovanny envisioned a march through the neighborhood for unity and peace. Someone wanted a plaque for Manny. Someone else thought we could plant and dedicate a tree. We had been in the process of getting some trees donated to the school, and suddenly from somewhere came the idea to build a park next to the school, and call it Unity Park. The meeting dispersed as quickly as it had formed. We had our idea and our project.

Two days after Manny's death, the alumni club was scheduled to go on its fall alumni leadership training weekend trip. It was also an open school day, so the first floor was flooded with students and parents. No one on my trip roster was in sight and it was getting late, so I began my search through the building. As I raced down the deserted second-floor hall, I spotted Walter's tall, lean body standing still as if suspended in time. I had never seen him so glazed. This mature, wise, caring Nicaraguan was using every bit of spiritual strength to keep himself against the wall. He described to me vividly and with such control the anger he was feeling. He was thinking of his younger brother who had died in Nicaragua from a knife attack that had been intended for Walter. And now he was not sure he was going to be able to keep himself from doing something stupid, from doing what he felt the police were not doing, from doing something, anything, for Manny.

Suddenly Carmen appeared, white faced and dry skinned. They were shooting on her block again. She shook me, shrieking that she could not find Angel, her brother, and that her mother was hysterical and on her way to school wanting to speak with me. And Rey's mom was already standing right next to me red faced and red eyed. Rey was cursing determined threats for that one teacher failing him. I knew that, in reality, he was yelling at the image buried in his heart of those two human forms stabbing his best friend to death. This recent incident had brought the past back to the present.

Somehow, I managed an insufficient few words with each of them and tried to steer us toward the bus. I assured Mrs. Rodriguez that Rey would calm down and that I would talk to him about his class. I asked Carmen to start over and slowly explain what was happening, and I kept an eye on Walter. When we were finally on our way and settled into our seats, I suddenly felt overwhelmed by the question that had been racing through my mind and heart all day: What could I do? What can any of us do to make a difference here?

Our first objective was to get some trees into our park before the ground froze. As winter set in, however, we began to lose momentum, and I wondered how we would sustain the enthusiasm and commitment until May. Sometime in November, I dashed down from class to the art room five minutes late for our regular weekly meeting to find Carmen sitting alone with her notebook and pen. I joined her at the table.

"So," I said.

She looked up. "So, what should we do?"

"Let's have a meeting," I responded.

"Let's have a meeting," she replied. Carmen showed me all the ideas she had mapped out. She had lists of local organizations she thought we should contact, as well as outlines for possible events we could organize. Carmen was committed. It was hard to imagine that this articulate, bold, and savvy young woman was a fifteen-year-old who had seen her share of personal struggle and was constantly fighting to keep coming to school. Although we were both obviously discouraged, neither one of us was willing to admit it. We carried on, determined to keep the club alive, convinced that if we kept doing, others would soon follow.

After Carmen left, I sat for a moment and wondered what the dangers could be of remaining too positive. While believing in the importance of high expectations, I also knew that I must be realistic. I was happy to have helped her feel proud of herself, but I certainly did not want her and any others set up for failure. And, this was not meant to be my project. I began to feel haunted by this question of how hard to push, and how much to allow the process to flow from the students.

Perhaps it is just not possible to avoid the mid-November lull. No matter how much I focused on creating a rich, dynamic curriculum for my class, it always seemed to fall flat at this time of year. The club attendance had dwindled, and the class was bored. I was bored and boring. We had completed our introductions, in which they interviewed each other and wrote biographies; we had been on our first backpacking trip; we had written a group contract; we had begun our cultural studies, and they had completed interviews of their own families. Now, in desperation (and lethargy), I tried having them write about themselves; I tried discussions; I even tried my old standby—debates. In reality, there was little solid content, and there was neither a trip nor a project in sight. And, spring and Unity Week were still too far away to engage the alumni.

It is hard to disentangle the string of events that darkened that winter month. There was always so much to do in preparation for the end of the term. One of my partners, Stacey Lennard, and I spent many evenings after school hours reviewing lists, planning lessons, and commiserating. We became somewhat dependent upon these moments together. One night, her call to me at the Outward Bound office to confirm our plan included the report that Joey's younger brother had been murdered. I knew that she could hear the disbelief and despair in my silence by the way she gently asked if I still wanted to meet. Stacey knew just how much Joey meant to me. We teachers work hard to treat each individual student with the same amount of attention and care, and yet I cannot deny that some students manage to bury themselves so deeply inside.

Later that week, I greeted Joey outside the funeral parlor on 149th Street and Grand Concourse where he was waiting for his younger brothers. We stood together for nearly two hours, mostly in silence, as the usual thick afternoon traffic of vendors and shoppers moved past us. Joey was his stoic self. He shoved his hands deeply into the pockets of his baggy jeans, and continued to glance up and down the block as if hanging for the afternoon. When I asked him how he was and what had happened, he calmly described a complex tragic story of revenge, ending each chapter with "I'm okay." At one point he broke the silence to announce, "I don't want you to stay late today." We both paused, and he continued, "I don't want anything to happen to you." My first instinct was to assure him that I was fine, but I caught myself and instead asked what he meant. He told me that he expected his brother's murderers to show up that evening because his older brother's gang would be there. He expected trouble at his brother's wake. I wondered if he was exaggerating and was still tempted to tell him not to worry, but I just did not know. This was not my world. This young seventeen-year-old, who was comforted by my presence and my care, was now also my teacher and protector. In his few words to me, he managed to expose simultaneously the vast distance between us and the intimate connection.

I spent the rest of the afternoon sitting in a metal folding chair in front of the open coffin. Time seemed to stand still as family and friends moved in and out of the room. So many old, young faces hesitated at the threshold of the room as if unsure of reality. As one young man entered, I looked up to see David, who had been in my class two years earlier before being transferred to his third high school. I recalled how he often sat next to Marilyn in class. By the end of interviewing and writing biographies of each other, Marilyn had looked up and said, "I've sat next to David for two years, never knew his name, and was scared. I have found out that he wears leather, listens to heavy metal, and is a really nice guy." Now he was standing in the doorway of this small room. He seemed unsure of what to do, and then our eyes met. At that moment we saw we were unsettled but comforted by each other's presence. We both knew we belonged there.

Not surprisingly, Joey was around school even less than before.

Each day, I heard another story because each young person has a story to tell. But because of my students it seemed impossible for me to lose myself to despair. Their indefatigable spirit and our closeness as a community was the foundation of the park. One morning I pushed through the school's heavy, metal front door and walked right into Ramon's jubilant smile. He came gliding up and wrapped his arms around me. "Oh, Susan," he whispered in that gorgeous Dominican accent.

He began to escort me to my office, "Susan, you look tired. You work too much. How are you? Did I tell you . . .?" Ramon always had news that he dispatched with hushed intensity. His warmth was contagious. He led me up the stairs and right into "the desk mob." After two years of bureaucratic battles, I had procured a space for the program big enough to house an intimate miniclub. I said my hellos, letting the group of students know how sincerely good it was to see them. And before I could ask them where they were supposed to be, they assured me that Veronica had finished her test and Louis had been kicked out of science. After a long pause, Alex quickly added that he was on his way back to class. It was always tempting to let them stay; I sensed that they flocked here because they could find connection and caring. But I knew, and they knew, that they also had to hold each other accountable for all their other academic responsibilities.

At this time of year it was always hard to hold their attention. Fortunately, the urban exploration was on the calendar. In many ways it became a pivotal juncture of the curriculum—an opportunity to see the lessons of the course as relevant and real. I hoped that studying other communities would help us develop ideas for our project. We would search for examples of parks and murals, and meet with people who could be role models and inspire our work.

But it took a lot of convincing. Students wondered why we should bother wandering the streets of New York City, a place they knew and sometimes feared. On a school trip they assumed there was always the chance of danger or, worse, ridicule from strangers. The Lower East Side is demographically and physically similar to the South Bronx, but once we were there it was far enough away from home that we could enter with an explorer's perspective, both anxious and open.

I helped them find their way to a collection of murals known in the Lower East Side as "the protest murals," but when we arrived and found the gate locked, we just stood on the corner suddenly aimless. We had spent hours in class practicing approaching and interviewing people in the street, but still the students were hesitant and resistant about moving beyond our group. Garfield took the initiative. He walked toward a man sitting on a nearby stoop, while the rest of the group stood riveted, watching and waiting in awe. This is not something a young Black Jamaican man wearing baggy jeans and a baseball cap does outside of his own neighborhood in New York City. The time passed; Garfield continued talking with this man while the rest of us stared at Garfield. Eventually, he took his journal out and began writing. Then he and the man began walking back toward us. "This is David." Garfield introduced each of us, and then told us that David knew all about the neighborhood. He had been homeless for years, but had spent that time in the area, and even had a key to the park. He helped build it, organized a rally when city officials threatened to destroy it, and was continuing to watch over it. So, we followed David into his garden, and spent the next hour of this bitter cold December day standing beneath the huge mural hearing about his life and his views of the homeless situation and of the social and political history of the community.

Later, Hugo, who recently came to this country from El Salvador, captured the moment in writing. He was usually so quiet and shy. He rarely spoke or wrote in class, but now he responded to a phrase in the mural painted beneath a crystal ball: " 'La Lucha Continua' means that the struggle never ends. You always have to keep on fighting for a better future. Never give up in life. Always keep trying to be the best." This is why I leave the classroom with my students; I could never have planned this experience.

As we walked away and left David sitting on his bench, Garfield pulled on the "hoody" of his full-length Fat Goose jacket and wrapped his arm around Carmen's shoulders. For that hour none of us had noticed the cold.

What would we do in schools without the changing of the semesters? Each February brings the opportunity to reflect, to put the past in the past, and to start anew. Launching a new course and facing an unknown crowd can be daunting, but it also brings possibilities. Julio was back. By the end of the semester he was failing so badly that there seemed no need even to try, but now he could start again. Last semester's students were now alumni; the ground would be softening; May would be coming, and we had a project to plan.

We had three more days to come up with a press release. Unity Week, which we had been planning all year, was now only two months away. The public relations firm we had visited advised us to look through newspapers to analyze their coverage of the South Bronx, so I had come to the meeting loaded with the day's local press. We were determined to create a positive image of young people in the South Bronx. I reminded them of the task, suggested they gather in groups, and distributed the papers. It did not take long to realize that they were more interested in the sports results than in writing a press release. Not surprisingly, three of the six people who had been at the public relations meeting were not in class, and I had no idea whether anyone understood what we were doing. Louis was reading aloud the *Post*'s personal ads, and trying to set Rose up on a date. Rose was focused on visibly ignoring Louis. Alex and Orlando were engaged in a deep discussion of this week's hooky party, and the seniors sitting on the counter in the back of the room were planning their next road trip while fighting over a bottle of soda. And we had three more days to come up with a press release.

I circled the room, hoping that one-on-one attention would redirect the conversations. After I spent five minutes with Orlando and Alex, they seemed to be on the right track, so I moved on to Louis, Rey, and Jose. I continued around, but by the time I had returned to Alex, he glanced up with his puppy dog look and asked, "So what are we doing?" As my anxiety rose, my interactions became more and more directive. "Here, look through these articles and write down which stories say anything about you." By now, Rose was yelling at Louis to stop bothering her, loud bursts of emphatic commentary were coming from the counter crowd, and I realized I was almost putting the words in their mouths. As the noise escalated and the newspapers began to flutter through the room, I knew we had lost our purpose. This writing strategy was too much my own. So, was our vision of Unity Week merely mine?

Suddenly, my voice snapped, "Enough. That is enough. I've had enough." I will raise my voice on occasion when I think they need it, but it is rare that I am genuinely angry, and they know the difference. There was a stunned silence in the room as I went on demanding that they focus, and see that while they say they want the mayor at their event and their project in print, these things will happen only if they write a press release.

"Are you all thinking?" I said. "Do you realize that none of this is ever going to come together if you don't do it?" I tried to read the sensation of seriousness that lingered in the air. Were they smelling the fear beneath my anger? Were they experiencing how profoundly I cared about this project? Perhaps for the first time they were seeing a glimmer of doubt from me and this scared them. I wondered again if I had been too reassuring. I wanted to be a supportive, encouraging spirit, but had I also let them become dependent on my belief in them? How could I let my passion help them act, and realize what *they* could accomplish?

"Push the tables together," I commanded. Obviously, small groups were not working; we needed attention and a central focus. "We are going to do this right. And anyone who does not want to sit at the table and have a serious conversation can leave now." Their bodies expressed a bewildered disbelief. These were words of a kind that was almost never heard in this group. This was a place where everyone was always accepted and problems were worked through. We got angry with each other, we ignored each other, but we never locked anyone out. Perhaps none of us had realized how rare these words were until I had spoken them. Had I gone too far? How could I set standards, making it clear that certain behavior was unacceptable, while guaranteeing that every individual was embraced and knew it?

While we were all trying to comprehend the moment, I continued and suggested we needed to think again about why we had begun this project and what we were trying to accomplish. This would help us with our task, as well as with our understanding and commitment.

After a painful heavy pause, Rose looked up, "I don't think I really remember." Now we were getting somewhere.

After another thoughtful silence, Jose glanced across the table toward Rose, and whispered, almost as a question, "It started when Manny died."

Geovanny quickly added, "But that's not only why. We are doing this because there's too much violence."

Victor joined in, "I agree. I don't think we should focus on Manny."

Now Andre added, "We want the press to see what we are doing, that we are not all hoods and drug dealers. I'm tired of reading about negative images that merely create stereotypes. We have got to show the world who we really are."

Eventually, I suggested that someone start taking notes. Half an hour later, it was five o'clock and people had to leave. We still did not have a press release, but we seemed to have a new beginning. I wondered how often we would have to revisit this conversation. I wanted to be able to push the task through but *now* realized just how elusive this project was. We were acting on a blurry image of an event and a heartfelt commitment to an even vaguer notion: bringing people together.

The next day Rose came running down the hall. "Have you seen Cameron? He's got the press release. He wrote it, and the rest of us looked at it this morning." I was not sure which was more exhilarating, having a press release or seeing Rose's pride. Was she proud of Cameron, herself, the group, or the project? Somehow, in this moment, it was all the same.

At first we told stories to keep ourselves entertained, but eventually a silent fluidity set in. We paced from truck to park and back again with armload after armload of bricks. We had been to every vacant lot in the neighborhood determined to find the best materials for paving our path. Suddenly, however, something was not quite right. I was still hauling, but my companions were no longer with me; they had taken up the pose. They were at the entrance to our garden holding up the fence with their backs. I strutted up in my theatrical melodramatic way, defiantly crossed my arms, glared into their stern faces, and demanded to know what was happening. Geovanny let a smirk through, and reminded me, as if I had lost my senses, "Su, school's out. The guys are passing." How stupid of me; they could not be seen carrying a bunch of bricks. I went back to the truck and took another load into the park. I had to decide whether I should not push them and just respect their space. After all, they were doing this on their own time, in their own community.

I continued on to the truck, grabbed another pile, and was suddenly back in front of them placing bricks into their hands.

Geovanny pleaded, "Su."

Jose exclaimed in defeat, "Oh no."

I was viciously relentless. "Enter thy park with pride, gentlemen. Carry forth. Besides, you don't think that I'm unloading this whole truck alone, now, do you?" I think I got a smile out of both of them, and on we went.

Back in the park, Geovanny placed his hand on my shoulder. "You know, that was cruel and unusual punishment." I pleaded guilty and asked them how they thought we could make the park "cool" and ultimately get others involved. I quickly added, "And don't ask me because we all know I don't know anything about cool."

Alex confirmed, "Now that's the truth."

They looked at each other and away again. There was a stillness in the air until Geovanny motioned with an amused and knowing nod of his head. He was on his way back to the truck. And the work continued.

As the semester wore on, and there was more to do with even less time in which to do it, a process and pattern began to emerge. Slowly, each individual seemed to find his or her place, his or her personal way to contribute to the whole. One day stands out as remarkably typical. During second period, Veronica sifted through seed catalogues, waiting for Rose to appear for confirmation of her choices, and Rey kept us entertained with stories about his dreams while he drafted designs for posters. Garfield floated through with his beautiful wide smile and his notes from his most recent interview. Garfield rarely came to meetings but had decided to be our documenter. He was gathering the school's view of violence in the community, and of what Unity Week could mean. And Joey was around even when he was not around. After weeks away he finally approached me to ask if he could go on our weekend retreat to plan Unity Week. Since then Joey had become our informal—and charismatic—school public relations man.

That afternoon, Carmen opened the meeting. "I don't think we have time for an activity today. So, let's do a personal check-in, hear from each of the committees, and then get to work." Orlando reported that the public relations committee now had a press release, thanks to Cameron, but needed to finish the letter of invitation. A roaring round of "Go Cameron, go Cameron!" broke out, managing to get an embarrassed smile out of him. Orlando added that they also needed to know from the events committee whom they were inviting. The room was full, and they were now battling to hold attention.

Carmen announced from the front, "Hey, we need quiet here."

Louis grumbled, "Who made you queen?" and settled down.

Carmen assured the public relations people that they would have their list by tomorrow. "We are going to the borough president's office today. Who's coming with me?"

Alex jumped, "I'll go."

But Veronica quickly reminded him, "No, Alex, you have to stay. You're part of the park committee." Bodies and voices began drifting around the room, but eventually everyone settled somewhere.

Orlando, Victor, Larry, and Rose were huddled over their letter of invitation, intent on forming every phrase and placing every period perfectly. Carmen, Michelle, and Joey were headed across town. Rey and the other artists were already in the cafeteria with Stacey working on the mural. They now had a design showing the power of people working together to save the earth from the forces of evil. On one side some students drafted dark images, while on the other side others painted the faces of people pulling a rope wrapped around a drawing of the globe that floated in the center of the mural.

The video committee was planning its interview questions while Robert, who has no patience for meetings or classes, was showing Jackie how to use the video camera. He had found what he was good at. Jose Vega, who rarely says a word in class, was back in the path where he had now been every afternoon for weeks, even on the days when no one else showed up. His father had just arrived with his truck in order to take the path builders to another lot full of good bricks. The park committee, Louis, Jose, Angel, Jose B., Veronica, Alex, and others, was hauling wheelbarrows, shovels, and the hose out into the garden. A supply of plants had come in, and there was a lot to be done.

That day I wandered through all the activity in awe. This was not just an extracurricular activity; this was social studies, English, math, science, and art. As during every afternoon class, the sound of chaos echoed through the halls, and yet there was focus, direction, and resolve to these words.

"We need more gloves."

"Where's the fire hydrant key?"

"Hey, we need some quiet here, we're trying to write."

"Pass me the chips."

"Ask Rey, he watered the garden last."

"Do we have to plant all of these today?"

"We don't have much time left."

At 3:10 P.M., as school was letting out and the crowds were storming by, the life in the park could not be ignored.

"Wait, I want to dig."

"But the guys are waiting at the corner."

"I want to dig."

"So?"

"I'll see you. Hey, where can I get a shovel?"

Later, Alex kept repeating, "This guy just came up and asked if he could help. No one has ever come up to me in the South Bronx before and introduced himself."

By 6:30 P.M., most of the activity was over for the day, and the remaining few students were in the art room coiling the hose. I stepped outside to do one last check for tools before closing the building and was stopped by the orange glow that lingers at the end of a hot bright day. I was captivated by the view of the sky, remarkably expanded by the number of vacant lots, and of the small square of land that suddenly had become a garden. And then I spotted Joey. All I could see through the blur in my eyes was the deep orange haze and the outline of Joey's body crouching down in the dirt teaching his two younger brothers, ages six and eight, how to plant a flower.

Eventually adrenaline, momentum, and a kind of wild, blind passion took over. I no longer had any idea who was doing what. I spent hours writing, checking, and rewriting lists, and things seemed to be happening. Garfield was selling T-shirts; Rey was always painting; Louis was putting up posters—where posters should not dare to go—Carmen was relentlessly planning; everyone was everywhere.

When everything was finally ready—the helium tank had been picked up, the platforms had been carried into the field, the extension cord long enough for Angel to set up his music had been found, the tables had arrived, the people had gathered—Carmen took her place where she belonged, behind the lectern, and opened our ceremony, "No one could ever believe how my home, the South Bronx, could be filled with goodness. But the so-called hoods, underprivileged, and troublemakers have created this Unity

Park." She went on to outline the history of our project and then introduced Joey.

"Outward Bound has helped me develop the interest in helping others and the community," Joey began. "Like many teenagers, I was into guns, drugs, gangs, and many other things that describe youth as hoodlums. Living in the streets, I also know what it feels like to lose a friend. I have lost so many friends that my fingers and toes aren't enough to count them all, including the life of my sixteen-year-old brother. There have been many times that I felt suicide was my only solution, but I found myself crying instead of going through with it. This is why I got involved in this project, Unity Week, because even though things don't always work out for me, I can help others and that makes me feel good. Seeing everyone here makes me happy because you are here to help fight the stereotypes of Blacks and Hispanics, and most of all to unite as one. I myself, being both Puerto Rican and Italian, represent that unity. And we have events like this one so that we can resort to other things besides selling drugs and killing. It's been said, but we must realize that we are the teachers of our next generation. It is our responsibility . . . Let me leave you with this: there is no feeling like the feeling of success, and right now I feel great."

After a moment of silence, we unveiled the mural, cut the ribbon, and finally invited our guests to join us in one large circle. Sales had soared, and every person present had on one of our T-shirts with our logo, a pattern of hands clasping arms. Students, teachers, parents, the man from the Flats Fixed place across the street, the woman who runs the party store down the block who donated the balloons, somebody's mom who baked a beautiful cake, Jose's dad, Carmen's mom, Outward Bound board members, all formed a ring of Unity Week T-shirts within our park. The press had not shown up after all, but it did not seem to matter. There was nothing planned for this moment, and when the crowd quieted down, Ray, who had spent so many hours working on the mural that now hung above us, remarked that while this picture showed people coming together, and while the park was a symbol of unity, it was in the process of creating this symbol that we had found unity. Then Garfield leaned his head forward and softly added, "We have met our challenge. We have made the circle bigger."

Expeditionary Learning
Outward Bound®
DESIGN PRINCIPLES

Learning is an expedition into the unknown. Expeditions draw together personal experience and intellectual growth to promote self-discovery and construct knowledge. We believe that adults should guide students along this journey with care, compassion, and respect for their diverse learning styles, backgrounds, and needs. Addressing individual differences profoundly increases the potential for learning and creativity of each student.

Given fundamental levels of health, safety and love, all people can and want to learn. We believe expeditionary learning harnesses the natural passion to learn and is a powerful method for developing the curiosity, skills, knowledge and courage needed to imagine a better world and work toward realizing it.

1. THE PRIMACY OF SELF-DISCOVERY
Learning happens best with emotion, challenge and the requisite support. People discover their abilities, values, "grand passions," and responsibilities in situations that offer adventure and the unexpected. They must have tasks that require perseverance, fitness, craftsmanship, imagination, self-discipline and significant achievement. A primary job of the educator is to help students overcome their fear and discover they have more in them than they think.

2. THE HAVING OF WONDERFUL IDEAS
Teach so as to build on children's curiosity about the world by creating learning situations that provide matter to think about, time to experiment, and time to make sense of what is observed. Foster a community where students' and adults' ideas are respected.

3. THE RESPONSIBILITY FOR LEARNING
Learning is both a personal, individually specific process of discovery and a social activity. Each of us learns within and for ourselves and as a part of

a group. Every aspect of a school must encourage children, young people, and adults to become increasingly responsible for directing their own personal and collective learning.

4. INTIMACY AND CARING

Learning is fostered best in small groups where there is trust, sustained caring and mutual respect among all members of the learning community. Keep schools and learning groups small. Be sure there is a caring adult looking after the progress of each child. Arrange for the older students to mentor the younger ones.

5. SUCCESS AND FAILURE

All students must be assured a fair measure of success in learning in order to nurture the confidence and capacity to take risks and rise to increasingly difficult challenges. But it is also important to experience failure, to overcome negative inclinations, to prevail against adversity and to learn to turn disabilities into opportunities.

6. COLLABORATION AND COMPETITION

Teach so as to join individual and group development so that the value of friendship, trust, and group endeavor is made manifest. Encourage students to compete, not against each other, but with their own personal best and with rigorous standards of excellence.

7. DIVERSITY AND INCLUSIVITY

Diversity and inclusivity in all groups dramatically increases richness of ideas, creative power, problem-solving ability, and acceptance of others. Encourage students to investigate, value and draw upon their own different histories, talents and resources together with those of other communities and cultures. Keep the schools and learning groups heterogeneous.

8. THE NATURAL WORLD

A direct and respectful relationship with the natural world refreshes the human spirit and reveals the important lessons of recurring cycles and cause and effect. Students learn to become stewards of the earth and of the generations to come.

9. SOLITUDE AND REFLECTION

Solitude, reflection, and silence replenish our energies and open our minds. Be sure students have time alone to explore their own thoughts, make their own connections and create their own ideas. Then give them opportunity to exchange their reflections with each other and with adults.

10. SERVICE AND COMPASSION

We are crew, not passengers, and are strengthened by acts of consequential service to others. One of a school's primary functions is to prepare its students with the attitudes and skills to learn from and be of service to others.

The above principles have been informed by Kurt Hahn's "Seven Laws of Salem," by Paul Ylvisaker's "The Missing Dimension," and by Eleanor Duckworth's *"The Having of Wonderful Ideas" and Other Essays on Teaching and Learning* (New York: Teachers College Press, Columbia University, 1987).

About Expeditionary Learning Outward Bound®

Expeditionary Learning Outward Bound, a New American Schools design, is a comprehensive school design for grades kindergarten-twelfth based on ten principles that grow in large part out of the experience of Outward Bound, a non-profit organization founded by educator Kurt Hahn in 1941. These design principles give schools a vision and a direction. They require greater continuity of relationships between students and teachers, drawing on the power of small groups; creating an in-depth and focused curriculum; and building strategic links between school and community.

In Expeditionary Learning schools, students spend most of each school day embarked on purposeful, rigorous "learning expeditions" that involve intellectual, service, and physical dimensions. Learning expeditions are in-depth studies of a single theme or topic, generally lasting four to nine weeks, that are the core of the curriculum. Each expedition revolves around projects and performances, which often take students outside of school to conduct fieldwork.

The Expeditionary Learning school "breaks the mold" in three dramatic and fundamental ways:

- Its hierarchy of values puts human beings' learning and character development together at the pinnacle.
- It requires the complete reorganization of time, space and relationships among people, across disciplines, between people and learning technology, and between the school and the community.
- Its high expectations for students' achievement and character development is manifested in a requirement for academically rigorous student demonstrations of intellectual, physical, and character competencies.

In Expeditionary Learning schools, classrooms are no longer silent, with rows of desks facing the blackboard. Instead, Expeditionary Learning schools eliminate the fifty-minute period and replace it with a schedule that accommodates hands-on, experience-based studies that engage students for weeks or even months. Tracking is eliminated, and students study with the same teacher or team of teachers for at least two years. Over time, this design builds community support for public education by offering parents and community members meaningful and rewarding involvement in students' intellectual and character development.

Expeditionary Learning's professional development activities emphasize professional and personal renewal, as well as preparing teachers to: work with students of differing ability levels; use students' ideas and understandings to guide teaching and curriculum development; reduce the amount of time spent lecturing or using textbooks; and use methods of inquiry to drive the curriculum and student project work.

For more information contact:

Expeditionary Learning Outward Bound
122 Mount Auburn Street
Cambridge, MA 02138
Phone 617-576-1260
Fax 617-576-1340
E-mail: info@elob.ci.net